NEW VANGUARD 319

BRITISH FRIGATES AND ESCORT DESTROYERS 1939–45

ANGUS KONSTAM   ILLUSTRATED BY ADAM TOOBY

OSPREY PUBLISHING

Bloomsbury Publishing Plc

Kemp House, Chawley Park, Cumnor Hill, Oxford OX2 9PH, UK

29 Earlsfort Terrace, Dublin 2, Ireland

1385 Broadway, 5th Floor, New York, NY 10018, USA

E-mail: info@ospreypublishing.com

www.ospreypublishing.com

OSPREY is a trademark of Osprey Publishing Ltd

First published in Great Britain in 2023

A catalogue record for this book is available from the British Library.

ISBN: PB 9781472858115; eBook 9781472858122
ePDF 9781472858092; XML 9781472858108

23 24 25 26 27 10 9 8 7 6 5 4 3 2 1

Index by Alan Rutter
Typeset by PDQ Digital Media Solutions, Bungay, UK
Printed and bound in India by Replika Press Private Ltd.

Osprey Publishing supports the Woodland Trust, the UK's leading woodland
conservation charity.

To find out more about our authors and books visit

www.ospreypublishing.com. Here you will find extracts, author
interviews, details of forthcoming events and the option to sign up for our
newsletter.

All photos courtesy of the Stratford Archive

Title page image: please see caption on page 10.

CONTENTS

BRITISH FRIGATES AND ESCORT DESTROYERS 1939–45

INTRODUCTION

In September 1939, Britain was plunged into a new world war, and it became clear that once again Germany would use its growing fleet of U-boats to prey on Allied shipping. The British Admiralty found itself desperately short of escort vessels to protect its convoys. Fortunately, a number of escort destroyers were on the stocks, a new breed of warship purpose-built for this vital role. While the 'Lend-Lease' programme saw the transfer of hundreds of old warships from American to British service, this alone wasn't enough. Fortunately, shipyards in Britain and the Commonwealth began building their own escort vessels, to help fill the void. Many of these types were escort destroyers and frigates.

The escort destroyer (known as the destroyer escort in the US Navy) was essentially a small destroyer, where speed and anti-surface weaponry were sacrificed in order to make a more potent anti-submarine and anti-aircraft warship. The first of these had been ordered before the war began, and began entering service in 1940. In all, a total of 86 of them were built. In 1943, the first 'frigates' joined the fleet, a name adopted from the fast, powerful cruisers of the Age of Fighting Sail. Modern frigates, though, were essentially small escort destroyers, designed so they could be built quickly in civilian shipyards. Over a hundred of them were constructed during the war.

Together, these two types of escort vessels saw extensive service, where their range and seagoing qualities made them well suited to use in the Atlantic, the Arctic and the Mediterranean. They were also used to form hunting groups, and collectively they accounted for scores of German U-boats. Their arrival came at a critical time for the Royal Navy, while the Battle of the Atlantic was reaching its climax and losses in both merchant ships and escorts were mounting alarmingly. Almost overnight, these new escorts made their presence felt in the protection of these lifeline convoys.

This book will tell the story of these British escort destroyers and frigates, from the years shortly before the outbreak of World War II until the conflict's end. It is hoped that later volumes will fill in the gaps in the story of

The Hunt-class Type 2 escort destroyer HMS *Lauderdale* (L95), pictured in late 1942. She spent much of the year escorting North Sea convoys as part of the Rosyth Escort Force. The following year though, she was sent to the Mediterranean. Note the distinctive 'V' design on her forward superstructure.

Britain's wartime escorts, concentrating on US-built Lend-Lease warships and the smaller sloops and corvettes which played such a key part in the naval war.

DESIGN AND DEVELOPMENT

When war broke out in September 1939, the British Admiralty was well aware of the precarious situation it faced. The German Navy (the *Kriegsmarine*) had a small but growing U-boat arm, and it was expected that from the outbreak of hostilities these would prey on British merchant shipping. During the Great War, the Kaiser's U-boats had come close to strangling Britain's vital maritime lifeline. Now, with better boats and a bigger shipbuilding capability, this submarine force was potentially even more dangerous. To counter it, the Royal Navy needed escort vessels – lots of them. While a convoy system was introduced, the Admiralty found itself hard pressed to provide the warships it needed to protect these vital convoys. New escort vessels were desperately needed, even though these would take time to build. The question was, what type of escorts would best serve the wartime needs of the country?

Escort vessels

The Royal Navy already had a large fleet of destroyers. These versatile warships were initially designed to launch torpedo attacks on enemy battle fleets. Torpedo boat destroyers were then developed to protect the battle fleet from such attacks. By 1918, destroyers were increasingly being used as ocean-going escorts, protecting Allied convoys from U-boats. A destroyer therefore had a range of roles, so during the inter-war years the British mainly built 'general-purpose destroyers', which could fulfil all these tasks, as well as cope with the growing threat posed by aircraft. When war came, though, most of these destroyers served with the fleet, meaning they weren't always available as convoy escorts. An emergency destroyer-building programme was put in place, but it would take years for these new war-built destroyers to enter service. So the Admiralty had to look elsewhere for its escorts.

For the most part, the business of trade protection had been left to sloops, a term from the Age of Sail which had been reintroduced by the Royal Navy

One of the lookouts on an escort, using one of the depth-charge throwers on his ship's starboard aft waist to steady himself during the escort of an Atlantic convoy through the North-Western Approaches in 1943. Up to four of these launchers were mounted on either side of his ship, in addition to the two depth-charge racks mounted at the ship's stern.

during World War I. The first of these were minesweepers, but by the late 1930s a sloop was a small, rugged warship which was slower than a destroyer and lacked its weaponry, but was well suited to convoy protection. These proved invaluable, particularly during the opening year or so of hostilities, before other anti-submarine warfare (ASW) warships could enter service. Although more sloops would be built during the war, including the excellent Black Swan class, the Admiralty opted for other types of escort vessel to bulk out its fleet.

The corvette was another abandoned naval term from the Age of Sail, which was now applied to a small, robust, purpose-built escort vessel. The corvette's hull was based on that of a Norwegian whaler, designed to be strong and able to cope with bad weather. While relatively slow and lightly armed, the corvette proved to be a reliable and effective escort vessel. Above all, its deliberately simple design drew on existing civilian shipbuilding techniques and parts, so it could be built quickly by small shipyards, and in large numbers. The first of these would enter service during 1940, and would serve the Admiralty's needs until larger and more effective warships could be built.

As a stopgap, the Admiralty turned to its World War I-era V&W-class destroyers. These should really have been taken to the breaker's yard years before, but over 40 of them survived in various reserve capacities. These were now hurriedly converted into long-range escorts and anti-aircraft destroyers, both of which could protect ocean-going convoys, and into short-range escorts to protect coastal convoys. Then, from September 1940, up to 50 equally aged American destroyers were provided to the Royal Navy under the Lend-Lease programme, although it would take time for these to enter service. These too provided Britain with a vital stopgap. However, it was clear that the Royal Navy would need more escorts – ones which were better suited to the challenges of modern anti-submarine warfare. Consequently, they would turn to two new types of ASW warships, which in time would help turn the tide of the war against the U-boats.

The escort destroyer

In September 1938, the Munich Crisis highlighted both the likelihood of war with Germany and Britain's lack of military preparedness. Fortunately for the Royal Navy, this led to the release of funds for rearmament. The Admiralty considered where these funds were best allocated. A new emergency destroyer-building programme was begun, while other larger warships were also ordered. This still left the problem of the provision of escorts, so Admiral Sir Roger Backhouse, the First Sea Lord, asked the Director of Naval Construction (DNC), Sir Stanley Goodall, to develop plans for a small destroyer to be used primarily for escort work. By the end of September, Backhouse was presented with two sets of sketch plans for a fast escort, one incorporating torpedo tubes and the other with these left out.

HMS *Liddesdale* (L100), a Type 2 Hunt-class escort destroyer which entered service in early 1941. After initial service in home waters, in 1943 she was sent to join Force H based in Gibraltar. She remained in the Mediterranean theatre until 1944, and with two other destroyers is jointly credited with the sinking of U-453 off Sardinia.

These fast escorts carried four 4in. high-angle (HA) guns capable of engaging both air and surface targets, and an adequate close-range anti-aircraft (AA) capability. They would be fitted with Asdic (sonar) and depth charges for ASW. While speed wasn't necessarily essential for convoy work, it helped when hunting U-boats. These ships would therefore be capable of making a minimum of 28 knots. Their hulls would also carry stabilizers to improve seaworthiness. The proposed design without the torpedoes was fitted with minesweeping gear instead. Standard displacement would be between 640 and 810 tons. The Admiralty stressed that it wanted these ships to be designed and built quickly, but also wanted them to be as cost-effective as possible. Despite this, the Admiralty rejected both sketches, and instead opted for a larger vessel altogether with three rather than two gun mountings as well as torpedoes.

In October 1938, the DNC and his team were given three months to produce detailed plans for these new fast escorts. The following month, funding was approved for ten of them in the 1938 naval programme, even though their design still hadn't been finalized. Ten more would follow in the 1939 programme. For the rest of the year, the design team thrashed out the myriad of details which needed to be overcome – everything from the provision of adequate crew quarters, magazine space and fuel tanks to the length and breadth of the hull, the fitting of the propulsion system and the selection of AA and ASW armament.

Time was of the essence, as it was expected that the first orders for these ships would be placed in January 1939. In the rush, though, a mistake was made in the design calculations which would have a profound effect on the performance of these new warships.

This error was not discovered before the first building contracts were placed, so it was only in early 1940, when the first three ships (*Atherstone*, *Eglinton* and *Hambledon*) were fitting out, that the

The launch of the escort destroyer *Atherstone* in Birkenhead, 12 December 1939. She was the firsrt of the Hunt class to be completed, despite initial problems with her stability. This was rectified by removing some of her weaponry, and this drastic modification was then applied to all of the remaining Type 1 Hunts still being fitted out.

HMS *Derwent* (L83), a Hunt Type 3, pictured breaking away after refuelling at sea, an operation she performed in August 1942 from the cruiser *Nigeria* before the start of Operation *Pedestal*, the largest Malta convoy mission of the war. The *Derwent*'s twin 21in. torpedo tubes can be seen amidships.

problem – affecting the vessels' stability – came to light. In essence, they were too top-heavy, meaning the finished vessels would be too unstable. Construction was halted on all ten ships until a solution was found; this involved losing one of the three twin-gun mountings, as well as the triple torpedo tube mounting. While this dealt with the stability problem, it also made the final ship much less potent than the Admiralty had envisaged. Still, work was resumed and the DNC vowed to remedy the stability problem before the second batch of ships was laid down.

By early 1940, it was felt that as these escort vessels represented a new type of warship, they should have an appropriately original name. Backhouse had first called them small destroyers, while Goodall labelled them fast escorts. The Admiralty linked the two names together to define them as escort destroyers. Later, the Americans, adopting a more cavalier approach to grammar, called them destroyer escorts. Either term reflected their design – they were small destroyers, and despite their reduction in armament they were also powerful escort vessels. By then, the first batch of escort destroyers under construction was referred to as the Hunt class. They were also sub-categorized as Type 1s, as the plan was to follow them with more similar ships, albeit ones which had been modified by the DNC to overcome the stability problem of the Type 1s.

In the end, these modifications had to wait. The first batch of nine vessels had been laid down in June 1939, by which time a second batch of nine had been ordered. Five more were ordered before the end of the year. By early 1940, when the stability problem came to light, the first nine of these had already been launched, so apart from their reduction in armament it was decided to complete these 23 Hunt (Type 1) escort destroyers, with the only changes being to their armament. Another Hunt-class batch had already been ordered, and the first eight of these had been laid down. Work on them was halted while still on the stocks, as the DNC's team modified their plans.

Hunt-class escort destroyers (Type 1) 23 vessels in group						
Vessel	Pennant no	Builder	Laid down	Launched	Commissioned	Fate
Atherstone	L05	Cammell Laird, Birkenhead	June 1939	December 1939	March 1940	Broken up, 1957
Berkeley	L17	Cammell Laird, Birkenhead	June 1939	January 1940	June 1940	Bombed and sunk off Dieppe, 19 August 1942
Blencathra	L24	Cammell Laird, Birkenhead	November 1939	August 1940	December 1940	Broken up, 1957
Brocklesby	L42	Cammell Laird, Birkenhead	November 1939	September 1940	April 1941	Broken up, 1968
Cattistock	L35	Yarrow, Clydeside	June 1939	February 1940	August 1940	Broken up, 1957
Cleveland	L46	Yarrow, Clydeside	July 1939	April 1940	September 1940	Wrecked on way to breakers, 28 June 1957
Cotswold	L54	Yarrow, Clydeside	October 1939	July 1940	November 1940	Used as a breakwater, Harwich, 1956, then broken up, 1957
Cottesmore	L78	Yarrow, Clydeside	December 1939	September 1940	December 1940	Sold to Egypt, 1950
Eglinton	L87	Vickers-Armstrong, Tyneside	June 1939	December 1939	August 1940	Broken up, 1956
Exmoor (i)	L61	Vickers-Armstrong, Tyneside	June 1939	January 1940	October 1940	Torpedoed and sunk by E-boat off Lowestoft, 25 February 1941
Fernie	L11	John Brown, Clydeside	June 1939	January 1940	May 1940	Broken up, 1956
Garth	L20	John Brown, Clydeside	June 1939	February 1940	July 1940	Broken up, 1958
Hambledon	L37	Swan Hunter, Tyneside	June 1939	December 1939	June 1940	Hulked, 1955, then broken up, 1957
Holderness	L48	Swan Hunter, Tyneside	June 1939	February 1940	August 1940	Broken up, 1956
Liddesdale	L100	Vickers-Armstrong, Tyneside	November 1939	August 1940	February 1941	Broken up, 1948
Mendip	L60	Swan Hunter, Tyneside	August 1939	April 1940	October 1940	To China, 1948
Meynell	L82	Swan Hunter, Tyneside	August 1939	June 1940	December 1940	To Ecuador, 1954
Pytchley	L92	Scotts, Greenock	July 1939	February 1940	October 1940	Broken up, 1956
Quantock	L58	Scotts, Greenock	July 1939	April 1940	February 1941	To Ecuador, 1954
Quorn	L66	Samuel White, Cowes	August 1939	March 1940	August 1940	Sunk by explosive motorboat off Normandy, 3 August 1944
Southdown	L25	Samuel White, Cowes	August 1939	July 1940	November 1940	Broken up, 1956
Tynedale	L96	Stephens, Clydeside	July 1939	June 1940	November 1940	Torpedoed and sunk by U-boat off Bougie, 12 December 1943
Whaddon	L45	Stephens, Clydeside	July 1939	July 1940	February 1941	Broken up, 1959

NB (i) indicates there was more than one vessel with the same name (usually when the earlier one was sunk).

Ultimately, this involved widening the beam of these ships by 30in. (76cm). For the ships which were already laid down, this was done by kippering – adding extra hull plates on either side of the keel plate.

For the next 22 Hunt Type 2s, laid down between March and October 1940, and for the two which followed in early 1941, the builders simply followed the revised plans produced by the DNC. The result was that the Type 2 Hunts were now stable enough to carry the third twin 4in. gun mounting. In the Hunt Type 1s, the space where it should have been carried was filled by the quadruple 2-pdr 'pom-pom'. Now, in the Type 2s, the third gun was mounted where it should have been, on top of the aft superstructure. The

HMS *Avon Vale* (L06), a Hunt-class Type 2, pictured at anchor off Portsmouth in May 1944 during preparations for Operation *Overlord* – the invasion of Normandy. This photograph provides a clear view of her 2-pdr bow chaser, together with her Type 291 radar at her foremast, a 'HuffDuff' HF/DF radio direction finder array atop of the stumpy mainmast and Type 271 in the large lantern housing just forward of it.

'pom-pom' was then moved to its originally planned position abaft the funnel. By the time these Hunt Type 2s were fitting out, better radar sets and light AA guns were available, so these were added before the ships entered service.

The first of the Hunt-class (Type 1) escorts – *Atherstone* – entered service in March 1940. The rest would follow between May and December, although four were only commissioned early the next year. By then, the initial Type 2s were being commissioned, with the bulk of them entering the Royal Navy during the second half of 1941. The rest would follow during the first half of 1942. However, three of them (*Bedale*, *Oakley* (i) *and Silverton*) would join the Polish Navy rather than the British fleet.

A HUNT-CLASS ESCORT DESTROYERS, TYPES 1 & 2

1. HMS *Atherstone* (L05) c.1942. In March 1940, HMS *Atherstone* became the first of the Hunt-class escort destroyers to enter service. The stability problems discovered during her fitting out had led to the completion of *Atherstone* and her Type 1 sister ships being halted until the issue was addressed by removing some of her armament. Once in service, *Atherstone* proved a useful addition to the fleet, serving first in the English Channel and then the North Sea, before being redeployed to the Mediterranean in March 1943. She remained in the theatre for the remainder of the war, spending the last six months of the conflict in the Adriatic. This shows her as she appeared in early 1942, when her primary task was protecting coastal convoys from attacks by German E-boats. She carries a Type 286 radar at her masthead and a single 2-pdr in her bow, used as a point-defence weapon against E-boats.

2. HMS *Avon Vale* (L06), c.1942. Similarly, HMS *Avon Vale* was the first Type 2 Hunt to be commissioned, joining the Home Fleet in February 1941. She was initially used as an escort vessel in the North-Western Approaches, but in the summer of 1941 was redeployed to Gibraltar to escort Malta convoys as well as ones between Britain and Gibraltar. By the end of the year, she was attached to the Mediterranean Fleet based in Alexandria, and saw extensive service in operations designed to support the Tobruk garrison. She sustained damage in the Second Battle of Sirte and returned home for repairs. She returned to the Mediterranean, and apart from a refit and a brief participation in the D-Day landings, remained in the Mediterranean theatre until the end of the war. This shows her in the striking splinter camouflage scheme she sported during the Sirte battle. She carries a Type 286 radar on her foremast and a HF/DF array on a stumpy mainmast, in addition to a Type 285 fire control radar abaft her bridge. By the end of the year, the Type 286 set was replaced by the superior Type 291.

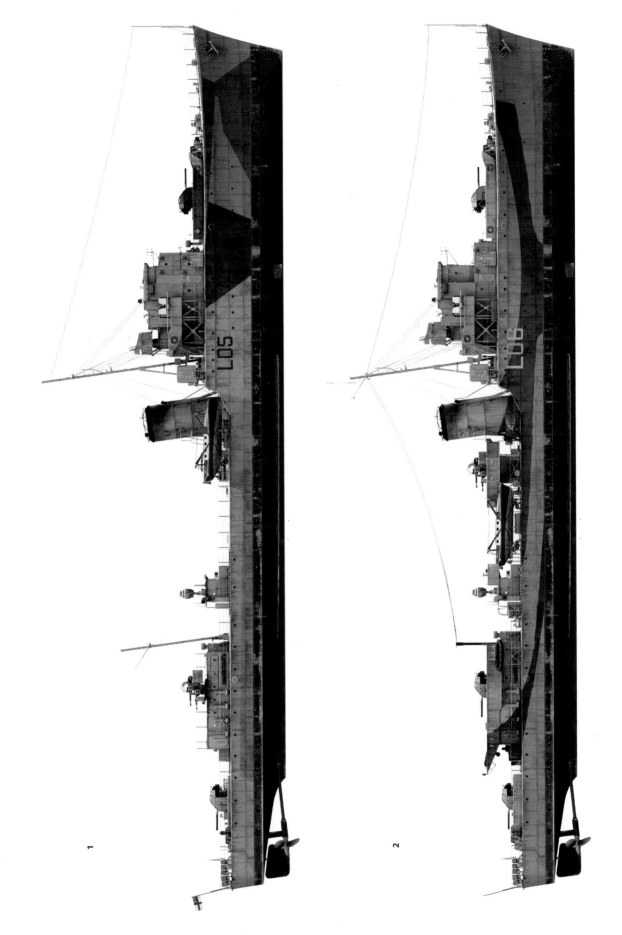

1

2

Hunt-class escort destroyers (Type 2) 30 vessels in group

Vessel	Pennant no	Builder	Laid down	Launched	Commissioned	Fate
Avon Vale	L06	John Brown, Clydeside	February 1940	October 1940	February 1941	Broken up, 1958
Badsworth	L03	Cammell Laird, Birkenhead	May 1940	March 1941	August 1941	To Norway, November 1944, as *Arendal*
Beaufort	L14	Cammell Laird, Birkenhead	July 1940	June 1941	November 1941	To Norway, 1952
Bicester	L34	Hawthorn Leslie, Tyneside	May 1940	September 1941	May 1942	Broken up, 1956
Blackmore	L43	Stephens, Clydeside	February 1941	December 1941	April 1942	Sold to Denmark, 1952
Blankney	L30	John Brown, Clydeside	May 1940	December 1940	April 1941	Broken up, 1959
Bramham	L51	Stephens, Clydeside	April 1941	January 1942	June 1942	To Greece, March 1943, as *Themistocles*
Calpe	L71	Swan Hunter, Tyneside	June 1940	April 1941	December 1941	To Denmark, 1952
Chiddingfold	L31	Scotts, Greenock	March 1940	March 1941	October 1941	To India, 1954
Cowdray	L52	Scotts, Greenock	April 1940	June 1941	July 1942	Broken up, 1959
Croome	L62	Stephens, Clydeside	June 1940	January 1941	June 1941	Broken up, 1957
Dulverton	L63	Stephens, Clydeside	July 1940	April 1941	September 1941	Bombed and sunk in Aegean, 13 November 1943
Eridge	L68	Swan Hunter, Tyneside	November 1939	August 1940	February 1941	Constructive loss after being torpedoed by Italian MTB off Egyptian coast, 29 August 1942
Exmoor (ii)	L08	Swan Hunter, Tyneside	June 1940	March 1941	October 1941	To Denmark, 1952
Farndale	L70	Swan Hunter, Tyneside	November 1939	September 1940	April 1941	Broken up, 1962
Grove	L77	Swan Hunter, Tyneside	August 1940	May 1941	February 1942	Torpedoed and sunk by U-boat off Sollum, 12 June 1942
Heythrop	L85	Swan Hunter, Tyneside	December 1939	October 1940	June 1941	Torpedoed and sunk by U-boat off Bardia, 20 March 1942
Hursley	L66	Swan Hunter, Tyneside	December 1940	July 1941	April 1942	To Greece, December 1943, as *Kriti*
Hurworth	L84	Vickers-Armstrong, Tyneside	April 1940	April 1941	October 1941	Mined and sunk in Aegean, 22 October 1943
Lamerton	L88	Swan Hunter, Tyneside	April 1940	December 1940	August 1941	To India, 1953
Lauderdale	L95	Thornycroft, Southampton	December 1939	August 1941	December 1941	To Greece, 1946
Ledbury	L90	Thornycroft, Southampton	January 1940	September 1941	February 1942	Broken up, 1958
Middleton	L74	Vickers-Armstrong, Tyneside	April 1940	May 1941	January 1942	Hulked, 1955, then broken up, 1957
Oakley (ii)	L98	Yarrow, Clydeside	August 1940	January 1942	May 1942	To Germany, 1958
Puckeridge	L108	Samuel White, Cowes	January 1940	March 1941	July 1941	Torpedoed and sunk by U-boat off Gibraltar, 6 September 1943
Southwold	L10	Samuel White, Cowes	June 1940	May 1941	October 1941	Mined and sunk off Malta, 24 March 1942
Tetcott	L99	Samuel White, Cowes	July 1940	August 1941	December 1941	Broken up, 1956
Wheatland	L122	Yarrow, Clydeside	May 1940	June 1941	November 1941	Broken up, 1959
Wilton	L128	Yarrow, Clydeside	June 1940	October 1941	February 1942	Broken up, 1959
Zetland	L59	Yarrow, Clydeside	October 1940	March 1942	June 1942	To Norway, 1954

This system of overlapping both designs and phases of construction was continued for the Hunt-class (Type 3) vessels. Thirty of these were approved in the 1940 programme, and the first of them was laid down as early as August 1940, before the bulk of the Type 1s had been commissioned into service. Essentially, these were repeats of the Hunt-class (Type 2), although advocates of the torpedo had encouraged the Admiralty to change the design somewhat. Now, the 'Y' gun, the twin 4in. mounting on the aft superstructure, was removed, and a single twin torpedo tube mounted in its place between the superstructure and the funnel. Some of the vessels were earmarked for service in the Far East (*Easton*, *Haydon*, *Melbreak* and *Talybont*). Two of the 1940 programme were fitted with a 40mm Bofors gun in front of the bridge, in lieu of the 20mm Oerlikons mounted on the bridge wings.

In all, 22 Type 3s would be commissioned into the Royal Navy, while six more would be transferred to the navies of Britain's allies – Greece, Norway and the Free French.

That left two of the 1940 programme of escort destroyers unaccounted for. Instead of following the others, these would be built to a completely new design. In the early autumn of 1938, when the Hunt class was first conceived,

HMS *Badsworth* (L03), a Hunt Type 2, entered service in the summer of 1941, and for the most part was deployed as a convoy escort in the North-Western Approaches – to the west of Ireland, as well as in the Arctic and Mediterranean. In August 1944, she was transferred to the Norwegian Navy and renamed the *Arendal*.

Like many of her sister ships, HMS *Bleasdale* (L50), a Hunt Type 3, carried a single 2-pdr gun mounted in her bow. This bow chaser was primarily mounted in Hunts which operated in the North Sea and English Channel, as it was found the weapon proved really useful when engaging E-boats.

Hunt-class escort destroyers (Type 3) 21 vessels in group						
Vessel	Pennant no	Builder	Laid down	Launched	Commissioned	Fate
Airedale	L07	John Brown, Clydeside	November 1940	August 1941	January 1942	Bombed and sunk off Crete, 15 June 1942
Albrighton	L12	John Brown, Clydeside	November 1940	October 1941	February 1942	To Germany, 1958
Aldenham	L22	Cammell Laird, Birkenhead	August 1940	August 1941	February 1942	Mined and sunk in Adriatic, 14 December 1944
Belvoir	L32	Cammell Laird, Birkenhead	October 1940	November 1941	March 1942	Broken up, 1957
Blean	L47	Hawthorn Leslie, Tyneside	February 1941	January 1942	August 1942	Torpedoed and sunk by U-boat off Oran, 11 December 1942
Bleasdale	L50	Vickers-Armstrong, Tyneside	October 1940	July 1941	April 1942	Broken up, 1956
Catterick	L81	Vickers-Armstrong, Barrow	March 1941	November 1941	June 1942	To Greece, 1946
Derwent	L83	Vickers-Armstrong, Barrow	December 1940	August 1941	April 1942	Broken up, 1947
Easton	L09	Samuel White, Cowes	March 1941	July 1942	December 1942	Broken up, 1953
Eggesford	L15	Samuel White, Cowes	June 1941	September 1942	January 1943	To Germany, 1958
Goathland	L27	Fairfield, Clydeside	January 1941	February 1942	November 1942	Mined off Normandy and declared constructive loss, 24 July 1944
Haydon	L75	Vickers-Armstrong, Tyneside	May 1941	April 1942	October 1942	Broken up, 1958
Holcombe	L56	Stephens, Clydeside	March 1941	April 1942	September 1942	Torpedoed and sunk by U-boat off Bougie, 12 December 1943
Limbourne	L57	Stephens, Clydeside	April 1941	May 1942	October 1942	Damaged in action with German torpedo boats off Brittany and scuttled, 23 October 1943
Melbreak	L73	Swan Hunter, Tyneside	June 1941	March 1942	October 1942	Broken up, 1956
Penylan	L89	Vickers-Armstrong, Barrow	June 1941	March 1942	August 1942	Torpedoed and sunk by E-boat off Devon, 3 December 1942
Rockwood	L39	Vickers-Armstrong, Barrow	August 1941	June 1942	November 1942	Damaged by glider bomb in Aegean and declared constructive loss, 11 November 1943
Stevenstone	L16	Stephen White, Cowes	September 1941	November 1942	March 1943	Broken up, 1959
Talybont	L18	Stephen White, Cowes	November 1941	February 1943	May 1943	Broken up, 1961
Tanatside	L69	Yarrow, Clydeside	June 1941	April 1942	September 1942	To Greece, 1946
Wensleydale	L86	Yarrow, Clydeside	July 1941	June 1942	October 1942	Damaged in collision with landing ship, 21 November 1944, and not repaired, then broken up, 1946

designers at the Thornycroft shipyard in Southampton had submitted their own proposals to the First Sea Lord, at his request. At the time these had been rejected by the Admiralty as being too costly, as well as being slightly slower than it wanted. They were, though, the only plans which met the armament requirements of the Admiralty – three twin turrets plus torpedo tubes. By way of an experiment, two of these vessels, built to a revised plan, were ordered from Thornycroft at the end of 1940. Work on them began the following February, and the first of them would enter service a year later.

The Hunt-class Type 3 HMS *Derwent* (L83), preparing to refuel from the aircraft carrier HMS *Illustrious* off Madagascar in October 1942. The escort destroyer was en route to Alexandria by way of the Suez Canal to join the Mediterranean Fleet there.

Dubbed the Hunt-class (Type 4), the two Thornycroft boats were notably different from their predecessors. For a start they had a long foredeck, which ran all the way aft as far as the aft superstructure. They were also heavier, displacing over 1,500 tons fully laden, and were wider than the earlier Hunts. However, they carried three twin turrets and a triple 21in. torpedo mounting. They actually turned out to be the best-designed escort destroyers of the war, the long forecastle enabling them to cope with very bad weather. They did have problems though – they had minor stability problems, which left them rolling heavily in rough weather. Still, their design would influence the plans for several classes of post-war frigates and destroyers.

The real problem with the Hunt ships was that they had been designed to fulfil the Admiralty's specifications, and no more. In the end, none of them – save for the two Type 4s – could safely accommodate the armament

Hunt-class escort destroyers (Type 4) 2 vessels in group

Vessel	Pennant no	Builder	Laid down	Launched	Commissioned	Fate
Brecon	L76	Thornycroft, Southampton	February 1941	June 1942	December 1942	Broken up, 1962
Brissenden	L79	Thornycroft, Southampton	February 1941	September 1942	February 1943	Broken up, 1965

HMS *Brecon* was a Hunt-class Type 4, one of two enlarged Hunts built by the Thornycroft shipyard in Southampton. They were the most powerful Hunts afloat, carrying both three twin 4in. turrets and torpedoes. She entered service in early 1943, was deployed in the Atlantic, North Sea and Mediterranean, and ended the war in Singapore as part of the naval group there to accept the Japanese surrender of Malaya.

the Admiralty wanted, so their configuration had to be scaled down slightly. The trouble here was that space on board them was at a premium, the result of having to pack so much into a such a relatively small space. As a result, there was very little leeway for any growth in terms of modifications to the original design. Although a few extra light AA guns were added, and new sensors fitted, any more significant alterations were impossible. This meant that they had a relatively short span of usefulness for the Royal Navy, which, at the start of the post-war era, was keen to embrace new developments in weaponry and technology. Put simply, as new technology became available after the war, the Hunt-class escort destroyers rapidly became obsolete.

HUNT-CLASS ESCORT DESTROYERS, TYPES 3 AND 4

B

1. HMS *Albrighton* (L12), *c.*1942–43. In the spring of 1942, HMS *Albrighton* joined the 1st Destroyer Flotilla, which was deployed in the English Channel. For much of the year, this Type 3 Hunt was heavily engaged in the flotilla's running battles with German light forces and in attacks on enemy coastal convoys. In August, she and other Hunts supported the disastrous Dieppe raid, engaging coastal batteries and firing in support of the Allied troops ashore. After a brief trip to Gibraltar, escorting troopships bound for French North Africa, she returned to the Channel and resumed her harrying of German naval forces there. During the D-Day landings, she briefly served as a headquarters ship for landing craft. At the war's end, *Albrighton* was placed in reserve, and ironically was sold to the German Navy in 1957. This shows her as she looked during her Channel battles of 1942.

2. HMS *Brecon* (L76), *c.*1942–43. HMS *Brecon* was one of only two Type 4 Hunts, designed and built by Thornycroft. *Brecon* and *Brissenden* were larger and more potent than previous Hunts, with three twin 4in. guns and a three-torpedo launcher amidships. They also carried a more effective close-range AA armament than their predecessors, and with Type 285 fire control and Type 291 air/surface search radar a better suite of sensors too. To cap this, they had excellent seakeeping qualities. Their only drawback was their cost – hence the reason only two of them were built. *Brecon* served briefly with the Home Fleet before being transferred to the Mediterranean. She saw action during the landings in Sicily, Salerno, Anzio and southern France, and also participated in the sinking of a U-boat in the Aegean. In 1945, she was sent to join the Eastern Fleet, ending the war in Singapore. This shows her as she appeared in mid-1943, while serving off eastern Sicily and Salerno.

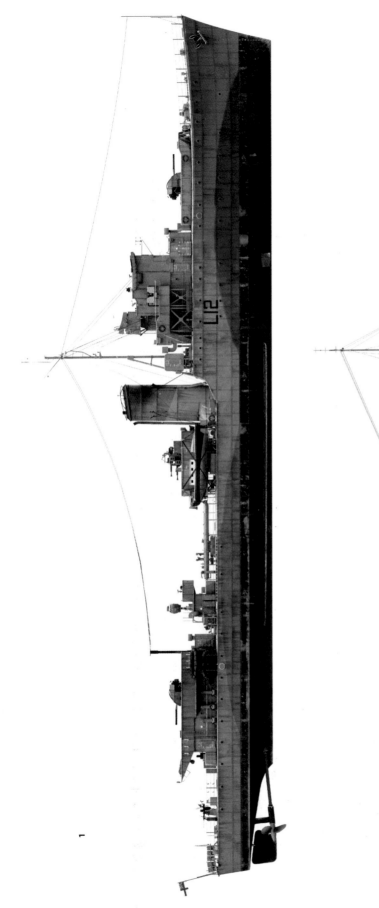

1

2

The frigate

While the escort destroyer would go a long way towards filling the numbers gap in ocean-going escorts, these alone would not be enough. They would take an average of a year to 18 months to build, and as they were ordered in groups, delivery would be even more spread out. The Admiralty needed a quicker solution, and ideally one where the escort vessel could be constructed in yards which weren't already building warships. The corvettes ordered from 1940 onwards were built in these smaller yards, and thanks to their largely civilian design they could be made by companies with little or no experience in the building of warships. Corvettes, though, were slow, so there was a clear need for something just as easy to produce but capable of greater speed and of handling rougher weather, and ideally provided with a heavier armament.

The DNC began the search by asking for the opinions of the shipbuilders who were actually building both escort destroyers and corvettes. Chief of these was William Reed of Smith's Dock Ltd in Teesside. This shipyard had first developed the corvette design, so Reed was considered ideally placed to offer the Admiralty advice on the building of larger escorts. He duly came up with the simple solution of using two of the propulsion systems fitted in Flower-class corvettes to create a two-screw rather than a single-screw vessel. Reed also suggested it should be around 320ft long, with a notable flare to the bow and sheer to the forecastle, to improve seaworthiness. The DNC, Sir Stanley Goodall, accepted this advice and came up with an initial design for this new type of vessel. Originally it was called a twin screw corvette, but while being built this new ship type was dubbed a frigate.

After the initial sketch plans were approved in late 1940, Goodall approached seven small shipbuilders to perfect certain parts of the overall design. Charles Hill developed the hull shape, Smith's Dock worked on the framing, Fleming & Ferguson the engine fittings and Henry Robb the mast and superstructure, while other yards dealt with the fixtures. The result was what became the River-class frigate, a much-improved version of the corvette, with everything Goodall wanted – improved armament, better speed, a more seaworthy hull and a markedly better range. The first of these, *Exe*, was laid down in the Scottish Fleming & Ferguson yard in May 1941. This was part of an initial batch of 12 vessels, ordered under the 1940 shipbuilding programme and laid down between May and September.

Like her sister ships, the Bay-class frigate HMS *St Austell Bay* (K634) was designed as an ASW escort and carried the Hedgehog, but her powerful armament of four 4in. QF Mk XVI HA guns, plus twin power-mounted 20mm Oerlikon and 40mm Bofors guns and a suite of air warning and fire control radars, made her a potent AA escort too. She was earmarked for AA escort service with the British Pacific Fleet but the war ended before she reached the Far East.

After being commissioned in October 1942 and completing her subsequent working-up, the River-class frigate HMS *Wear* (K230) was deployed in the North-Western Approaches. She spent almost a year operating as a convoy escort there before being redeployed to Gibraltar, where she resumed her escort role on the Gibraltar and Western Mediterranean convoys.

By mid 1941 another ten vessels had been ordered, these being laid down between October 1941 and June 1942. In all, 29 of this first group of River-class frigates were built, in ten different yards. The first of these new escorts, the *Rother*, built in Smith's Dock, entered service in April 1942. By the end of the year, she would be joined by 11 others. Fully laden, these frigates displaced over 1,800 tons but were capable of making 20 knots – a crucial four-knot edge over Flower-class corvettes. Armament was a pair of single 4in. guns, designed primarily to fire at U-boats, with 20mm Oerlikons as AA protection. Most importantly, as well as conventional depth charge racks and throwers, they carried the newly designed Hedgehog, a groundbreaking ASW weapon which could fire its mortar projectiles ahead of the warship.

These River-class frigates – named after rivers in the British Isles – proved so useful that a second, larger group of 30 vessels was ordered in the summer of 1941. The first of these, the *Swale*, was built in Bristol and commissioned in June 1942. These were repeats of the first group, except they carried a pair of twin 4in. mountings instead of single ones. Also, while the first group initially carried minesweeping gear, in the second group this was done away with, the space being used to carry more depth charges instead. There were other minor improvements too, including a greater fuel capacity – which meant a better range – less basic crew accommodation and improved sensors.

The River-class frigates proved so popular that others were built for service in the Australian and Canadian navies. Five of the British ships were transferred to other Allied navies before being commissioned, while eight more – built in Canada for the US Navy – were transferred into

The frigate HMS *St Brides Bay* (K600) was only commissioned in June 1945, and although earmarked to join the British Pacific Fleet she never saw active wartime service. She was, however, deployed off Korea in 1950 during the conflict there. This photograph gives a good indication of her sensors: a Type 285 fire control radar abaft her bridge, Type 276 target indication and 291 air search radars on her foremast, and HF/DF radio direction finding array on her stumpy mainmast.

River-class frigates (Group 1) 22 vessels in group

Vessel	Pennant no	Builder	Laid down	Launched	Commissioned	Fate
Ballinderry	K255	Blyth Shipbuilding, Blyth	November 1941	December 1942	September 1943	Broken up, 1961
Bann	K256	Charles Hill, Bristol	June 1942	December 1942	May 1943	To India, 1945
Chelmer	K221	George Brown, Greenock	December 1941	March 1943	September 1943	Broken up, 1957
Dart	K21	Blyth Shipbuilding, Blyth	September 1941	October 1942	May 1943	Broken up, 1957
Derg	K257	Henry Robb, Leith	April 1942	January 1943	June 1943	Broken up, 1960
Ettrick	K254	John Crown, Sunderland	December 1941	February 1943	July 1943	On loan to Canada, 1944–45, then broken up, 1953
Exe	K92	Fleming & Ferguson, Paisley	May 1941	March 1942	August 1942	Broken up, 1956
Itchen	K227	Fleming & Ferguson, Paisley	July 1941	July 1942	December 1942	Torpedoed and sunk by U-boat in Atlantic, 22 September 1943
Jed	K235	Charles Hill, Bristol	September 1941	July 1942	November 1942	Broken up, 1957
Kale	K241	A. & J. Inglis, Clydeside	September 1941	June 1942	December 1942	Broken up, 1957
Ness	K219	Henry Robb, Leith	September 1941	July 1942	December 1942	Broken up, 1956
Nith	K215	Henry Robb, Leith	September 1941	September 1942	February 1943	To Egypt, 1948
Rother	K224	Smith's Dock, Teesside	June 1941	November 1941	April 1942	Broken up, 1955
Spey	K246	Smith's Dock, Teesside	July 1941	December 1941	May 1942	To Egypt, 1948
Swale	K217	Smith's Dock, Teesside	August 1941	January 1942	June 1942	On loan to South Africa, 1945–46, then broken up, 1955
Tay	K232	Smith's Dock, Teesside	September 1941	March 1942	August 1942	Broken up, 1956
Test	K239	Hall Russell, Aberdeen	August 1941	May 1942	October 1942	Broken up, 1955
Teviot	K222	Hall Russell, Aberdeen	October 1941	October 1942	January 1943	On loan to South Africa, 1945–46, then broken up, 1955
Trent	K243	Charles Hill, Bristol	January 1942	October 1942	February 1943	To India, 1946
Tweed	K250	A. & J. Inglis, Clydeside	December 1941	November 1942	April 1943	Torpedoed and sunk in Atlantic by U-boat, 7 January 1944
Waveney	K248	Smith's Dock, Teesside	October 1941	April 1942	September 1942	Broken up, 1957
Wear	K230	Smith's Dock, Teesside	October 1941	June 1942	October 1942	Broken up, 1957

British service through the Lend-Lease programme. By the early summer of 1943, the initial group of these River-class frigates had entered service, proving highly useful as ocean-going escorts. Consequently, the Admiralty decided to order more of them. This latest batch would have a slightly improved design, as the DNC had now fully embraced the concept of mass-production. These new frigates would have prefabricated hulls, to encourage speedy building, and would carry another new ASW weapon, the Squid. Like the Hedgehog, this three-barrelled mortar projected some distance from the frigate, but unlike its predecessor it had a virtually all-round arc of fire, making it considerably more versatile. The Squid entered service in May 1943.

River-class frigates (Group 2) 27 vessels in group

Vessel	Pennant no	Builder	Laid down	Launched	Commissioned	Fate
Aire	K262	Fleming & Ferguson, Paisley	June 1942	April 1943	July 1943	To India, 1945, then wrecked off Singapore, 1946
Avon	K97	Charles Hill, Bristol	January 1943	June 1943	September 1943	To Portugal, 1949
Awe	K526	Fleming & Ferguson, Paisley	May 1943	December 1943	April 1944	To Portugal, 1949
Cam	K264	George Brown, Greenock	June 1942	July 1943	January 1944	Broken up, 1945
Deveron	K265	Smith's Dock, Teesside	April 1942	October 1942	March 1943	To India, 1945
Dovey	K523	Fleming & Ferguson, Paisley	March 1943	October 1943	February 1944	Broken up, 1955
Fal	K266	Smith's Dock, Teesside	May 1942	November 1942	July 1943	To Burma, 1948
Glenarm/Strule	K258	Henry Robb, Leith	July 1942	March 1943	July 1943	Renamed *Strule* 1 February 1944, to Free France September 1944 as *Croix de Lorraine*
Halladale	K417	A. & J. Inglis, Clydeside	June 1943	January 1944	May 1944	Sold to private buyer, 1949
Helford	K252	Hall Russell, Aberdeen	June 1942	February 1943	June 1943	Broken up, 1956
Helmsdale	K253	A. & J. Inglis, Clydeside	August 1942	June 1943	October 1943	Broken up, 1957
Lagan	K259	Smith's Dock, Teesside	January 1942	July 1942	December 1942	Torpedoed by U-boat in Atlantic and deemed constructive loss, 20 September 1944
Lochy	K365	Hall Russell, Aberdeen	February 1943	October 1943	February 1944	Broken up, 1956
Meon	K269	A. & J. Inglis, Clydeside	December 1942	August 1943	December 1943	To Canada, 1944–45, then broken up, 1966
Monnow	K441	Charles Hill, Bristol	September 1943	December 1943	May 1944	To Canada, 1944–-45, then to Denmark, 1945
Mourne	K261	Smith's Dock, Teesside	March 1942	September 1942	April 1943	Torpedoed and sunk by U-boat off Cornwall, 15 June 1944
Nadder	K392	Smith's Dock, Teesside	March 1943	September 1943	January 1944	To Pakistan, 1948
Nene	K270	Smith's Dock, Teesside	June 1942	December 1942	April 1943	To Canada, 1944–45, then broken up, 1955
Odzani	K356	Smith's Dock, Teesside	November 1942	May 1943	September 1943	Broken up, 1957
Plym	K271	Smith's Dock, Teesside	August 1942	February 1943	May 1943	To RNVR as drillship, 1948, then sunk in atomic test, Australia, 1952
Swale	K217	Smith's Dock, Teesside	August 1941	January 1942	June 1942	Broken up, 1955
Taff	K637	Charles Hill, Bristol	April 1943	September 1943	January 1944	Broken up, 1957
Tavy	K272	Smith's Dock, Teesside	October 1942	April 1943	July 1943	Broken up, 1955
Tees	K293	Hall Russell, Aberdeen	October 1942	May 1943	August 1943	Broken up, 1955
Towy	K294	Smith's Dock, Teesside	September 1942	March 1943	June 1943	Broken up, 1956
Usk (ii)	K250	Smith's Dock, Teesside	October 1942	April 1943	July 1943	To Egypt, 1948
Wye	K371	Henry Robb, Leith	November 1942	August 1943	February 1944	Broken up, 1955

HMS *Loch Fyne* (K429) joined the fleet in November 1944, and after VE Day took part in escorting of German U-boats from Norway to Britain. Her pennant number was changed to F429 in 1948 and she remained in service until 1963. At her masthead is the Type 277 radar, a combined surface and air search system introduced at the end of the war.

These improved versions of the River-class frigates were called the Loch class, with all vessels named after Scottish lochs. A total of 29 of them were built, four of which were transferred to the South African Navy. The first of the Lochs was *Loch Fada*, built on Clydebank, which was laid down in June 1943 and entered service the following April. She and her immediate successors had barely been put through their paces when a new group of frigates was ordered. These became the Bay-class frigates, 19 of which were built using the hulls of an additional batch of Lochs which the Admiralty decided would no longer be needed. The threat posed by enemy aircraft meant this new class of ships had an improved AA armament, but at the expense of their ASW capability. The first Bay-class frigates were laid down in April 1944, being commissioned into service from April 1945 onwards. A few, though, were not completed before the end of the war.

While Lend-Lease warships are not included in this survey, for the sake of completeness we need to mention the Captain-class frigates. These were

C RIVER-CLASS FRIGATES, GROUP 1 AND GROUP 2

1. HMS *Rother* (K224), c.1942–43. Launched in Teeside in late 1941, HMS *Rother* was commissioned into the Royal Navy the following April, making her the first of her class. She was described as a RN Group 1 River-class frigate, as her design had been altered slightly before a subsequent batch was ordered. As an ASW frigate, her primary offensive weapon was the depth charge, but significantly she carried a Hedgehog launcher on her forecastle, which gave her and her sister ships a game-changing advantage in the war against the U-boats. She saw service in the Atlantic before being sent into the Mediterranean in late 1942 as an escort for the Operation *Torch* convoys bound for French North Africa. She was then deployed as a convoy escort on the Britain to Gibraltar route, a task she performed for the remainder of the war, save for brief trips to the Indian Ocean and the Eastern Mediterranean. This shows her as she appeared in mid-1942, while operating in the Western Approaches. She carries a Type 286PU radar on her foremast and a Type 271 on her bridge.

2. HMS *Aire* (K262), c.1942–43. HMS *Aire* was a Group 2 River-class frigate. These differed only marginally from their predecessors, the only significant change being having their gun mounts replaced by the 4in. QF HA Mk XVI guns carried in the Hunts, and their associated Type 285 fire control radar. In October 1943, after working-up, she was assigned to convoy escort duties in the Atlantic, a task she continued until December 1944. This was followed by a two-month deployment as part of the 8th Escort Group in early 1945, followed by a return to convoy escort duties, this time in the North Sea. After Germany's surrender, *Aire* was sent to the Far East. The *Aire* is shown as she appeared in 1943, while serving in the Atlantic. Unusually, instead of a twin 4in. gun aft, she carries a single 12-pdr AA gun, augmenting two single power-operated 2-pdrs in a gun platform amidships, and single 20mm Oerlikons on her bridge wings. Her radar suite comprises Type 272 and Type 244 radars and a HF/DF array.

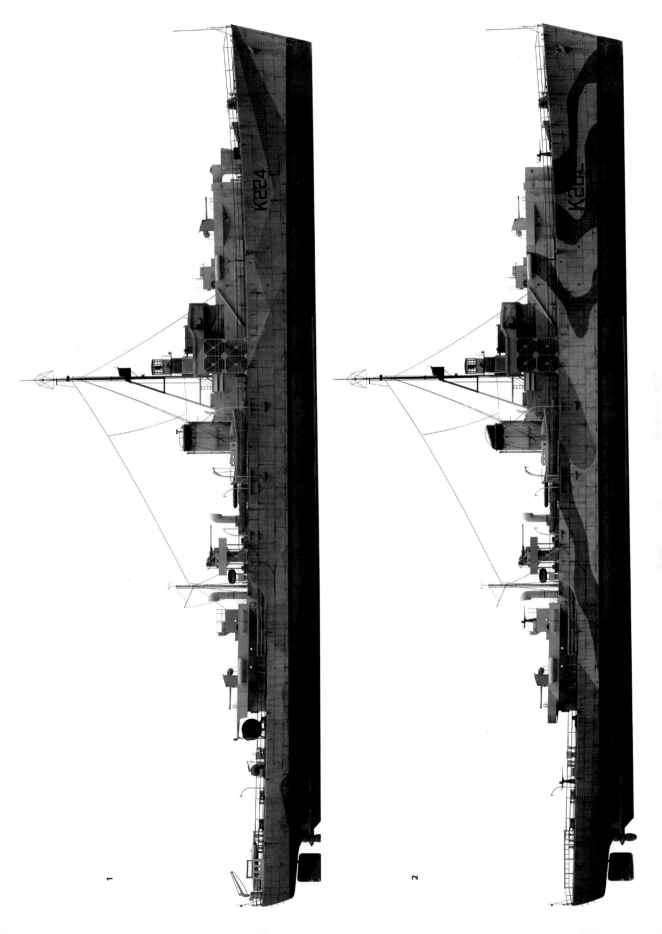

1

2

Loch-class frigates 25 vessels in class

Vessel	Pennant no	Builder	Laid down	Launched	Commissioned	Fate
Loch Achanalt	K424	Henry Robb, Leith	September 1943	March 1944	June 1945	To Canada, 1945–46, then to New Zealand, 1948
Loch Achray	K426	Smith's Dock, Teesside	December 1943	July 1944	February 1945	To New Zealand, 1948
Loch Alvie	K428	Barley, Curle & Co, Clydeside	August 1943	April 1944	June 1945	To Canada, 1944–45, then broken up, 1965
Loch Arkaig	K603	Caledon Shipbuilding, Dundee	November 1944	June 1945	November 1945	Broken up, 1960
Loch Craggie	K609	Harland & Wolff, Belfast	December 1943	May 1944	October 1944	Broken up, 1963
Loch Dunvegan	K425	Charles Hill, Bristol	September 1943	March 1944	June 1944	Broken up, 1960
Loch Eck	K422	Smith's Dock, Teesside	October 1943	April 1944	November 1944	To New Zealand, 1948
Loch Fada	K390	John Brown, Clydeside	June 1943	December 1943	April 1944	Broken up, 1970
Loch Fyne	K429	Burntisland Shipbuilding, Burntisland	December 1943	May 1944	November 1944	Broken up, 1970
Loch Glendhu	K619	Burnistland Shipbuilding, Burntisland	May 1944	October 1944	February 1945	Broken up, 1957
Loch Gorm	K620	Harland & Wolff, Belfast	December 1943	June 1944	December 1944	To Greece, 1961
Loch Insh	K433	Henry Robb, Leith	November 1943	May 1944	October 1944	To Malaysia, 1964
Loch Katrine	K625	Henry Robb, Leith	December 1943	August 1944	December 1944	To New Zealand, 1949
Loch Killin	K391	Burntisland Shipbuilding, Burntisland	June 1943	November 1943	April 1944	Broken up, 1960
Loch Killisport	K628	Harland & Wolff, Belfast	December 1943	July 1944	September 1945	Broken up, 1970
Loch Lomond	K437	Caledon Shipbuilding, Dundee	December 1943	June 1944	November 1944	Broken up, 1968
Loch More	K639	Caledon Shipbuilding, Dundee	March 1944	October 1944	February 1945	Broken up, 1963
Loch Morlich	K517	Swan Hunter, Tyneside	July 1943	January 1944	June 1945	To Canada 1944–45, then to New Zealand, 1949
Loch Quoich	K434	Blyth Shipbuilding, Blyth	December 1943	September 1944	January 1945	Broken up, 1957
Loch Ruthven	K645	Charles Hill, Bristol	January 1944	June 1944	October 1944	Broken up, 1966
Loch Skavaig	K648	Charles Hill, Bristol	March 1944	September 1944	December 1944	Broken up, 1959
Loch Shin	K421	Swan Hunter, Tyneside	September 1943	February 1944	October 1944	To New Zealand, 1948
Loch Tarbert	K431	Ailsa Shipbuilding, Troon	November 1943	October 1944	February 1945	Broken up, 1959
Loch Tralaig	K655	Caledon Shipbuilding, Dundee	June 1944	February 1945	July 1945	Broken up, 1963
Loch Veyatie	K658	Ailsa Shipbuilding, Troon	March 1944	October 1945	July 1946	Broken up, 1965

The River-class frigate HMS *Tay* (K232), named after the Scottish river, entered service in August 1942, initially serving as an escort in the Western Approaches before being redeployed to the Far East in mid-1943. In this immediate post-war view of her, she carries a Type 277 combined surface and air search radar abaft her bridge and a single 20mm Oerlikon mounted in her bow.

Bay-class frigates 19 vessels in class

Vessel	Pennant no	Builder	Laid down	Launched	Commissioned	Fate
Bigbury Bay	K606	Hall Russell, Aberdeen	May 1944	November 1944	July 1945	To Portugal, 1959
Burghead Bay	K622	Charles Hill, Bristol	September 1944	March 1945	September 1945	To Portugal, 1959
Cardigan Bay	K630	Henry Robb, Leith	April 1944	December 1944	June 1945	Broken up, 1962
Carnarvon Bay	K636	Henry Robb, Leith	June 1944	March 1945	September 1945	Broken up, 1959
Cawsand Bay	K644	Blyth Shipbuilding, Blyth	April 1944	February 1945	November 1945	Broken up, 1959
Enard Bay	K435	Smith's Dock, Teesside	May 1944	October 1944	January 1946	Broken up, 1957
Largo Bay	K423	William Pickersgill, Sunderland	February 1944	October 1944	January 1946	Broken up, 1958
Morecambe Bay	K634	William Pickersgill, Sunderland	March 1944	November 1944	February 1949	To Portugal, 1961
Mounts Bay	K627	William Pickersgill, Sunderland	October 1944	June 1945	April 1946	To Portugal, 1961
Padstow Bay	K608	Henry Robb, Leith	September 1944	August 1945	March 1946	Broken up, 1959
Porlock Bay	K650	Charles Hill, Bristol	November 1944	June 1945	March 1946	To Finland, 1962
St Austell Bay	K634	Harland & Wolff, Belfast	May 1944	November 1944	May 1945	Broken up, 1959
St Brides Bay	K600	Harland & Wolff, Belfast	May 1944	January 1945	June 1945	Broken up, 1962
Start Bay	K604	Harland & Wolff, Belfast	August 1944	February 1945	September 1945	Broken up, 1958
Tremadoc Bay	K605	Harland & Wolff, Belfast	August 1944	March 1945	October 1945	Broken up, 1959
Veryan Bay	K651	Charles Hill, Bristol	June 1944	November 1944	July 1945	Broken up, 1959
Whitesand Bay	K633	Harland & Wolff, Belfast	August 1944	December 1944	July 1945	Broken up, 1956
Widemouth Bay	K615	Harland & Wolff, Belfast	April 1944	October 1944	April 1945	Broken up, 1957
Wigtown Bay	K616	Harland & Wolff, Belfast	October 1944	April 1945	January 1946	Broken up, 1959

American-built Buckley and Evarts-class destroyer escorts, also known as the TE and GMT classes respectively. The US version of the escort destroyer was smaller than its British counterpart, so while the Americans called these vessels destroyer escorts (DEs), the British classified them as frigates. Some 78 of them were transferred to the Royal Navy from 1943–44 under the Lend-Lease programme. Once in British hands, they were modified slightly to better suit British needs and equipment. These Captain-class ships provided the Royal Navy with all the escorts it could need during the final years of the war – or rather all it could actually man.

Capabilities

These new escort destroyers and frigates were built to dramatically boost the number of escort vessels in the wartime Royal Navy. This meant that

As a Hunt Type 2, HMS *Farndale* (L70) was fitted with three twin 4in. mountings – one, 'A', forward, and 'X' and 'Y' aft. Her quadruple 2-pdr 'pom-pom' can be seen abaft her funnel. Atop her foremast is an array of Type 291 search radar, while abaft the bridge is the Type 285 fire control radar.

The Hunt-class Type 2 HMS *Calpe* (L71) without any number painted on her side, approaching the battlecruiser HMS *Renown* before refuelling from her in the Mediterranean during Operation *Torch* – the Allied invasion of French North Africa. The battleship in the background is HMS *Rodney*.

when they were designed, their primary role was seen as ASW vessels, which would protect convoys and even larger units of the fleet from attack by U-boats and – from June 1940 on – from Italian submarines as well. With an effective Asdic array and a potent ASW armament of depth charges, they could also be formidable U-boat hunters. If this had been the only role expected of them, then these little warships wouldn't have been expected to carry much in the way of surface weaponry, and certainly not torpedoes. A single 4in. gun or two would have sufficed to take on U-boats on the surface, supported by a small number of close-range AA weapons for the vessel's own protection. Yet while this might have been true of the Navy's new frigates, its escort destroyers were clearly designed to be much more versatile.

General capabilities

When first designed, it was intended that the Hunt class would carry six dual-purpose 4in. guns, capable of being used against surface targets and aircraft, supported by a simple but effective fire control system. It was also hoped that they would carry torpedoes, although thanks to design problems these were only fitted in the Type 3 and Type 4 Hunts. Thus, from the outset it was clear that the Admiralty wanted the Hunts to be more than just ASW escorts. The original intention was to build small destroyers, akin to the larger German torpedo boats then in service. When they entered service, they quickly proved just how handy and valuable they could be, and were used

D

LOCH- AND BAY-CLASS FRIGATES

The Loch and Bay classes of frigate were developments of the earlier River class, designed for mass production. The Rivers had used prefabricated parts to speed production, and here the two classes combined this with a common hull design. Apart from two of the Lochs, they also had identical propulsion systems. The main difference between the two classes was in armament – the Lochs emphasising ASW capability, carrying Hedgehog mortars and depth charges, while the Bays combined this in the shape of their Squid mortar with a potent AA capability.

1. HMS *Loch Eck* (K422), c.1944–45. HMS *Loch Eck* entered service in October 1944, and was assigned to the Londonderry Escort Group. She operated in the South-Western Approaches and the English Channel until January 1945, when she was transferred to Scapa Flow for service in the North-Western Approaches. Together with other escorts, she participated in the sinking of three U-boats off Shetland (U-989, U-1278 and U-1279). This shows her as she was during this final phase of the war, carrying a Type 277 radar atop her lattice foremast and a HF/DF array at the foremast peak.

2. HMS *Cardigan Bay* (K630), c.1944–45. As so many Loch-class frigates were ordered, 19 of them were converted while under construction to produce the Bay class, which combined AA and ASW capabilities. HMS *Cardigan Bay* (bottom) entered service after the end of the war in Europe, and although earmarked for service in the Pacific, the war ended when she was still in the Mediterranean. Instead, she was used to intercept immigrant ships bound for Palestine, one of which was the famous SS *Exodus*. This shows her as she looked in mid-1945, while based in Malta. As she was earmarked for the Pacific, her Squid mortars had been replaced by a Hedgehog and a twin 4in. Mk XVI mounting, augmenting her powerful close-range AA armament of two twin 20mm and two twin 40mm power mounts. She is fitted with a Type 271 radar at her masthead, as well as a Type 285 fire control radar, and a Type 293 projecting from her foremast.

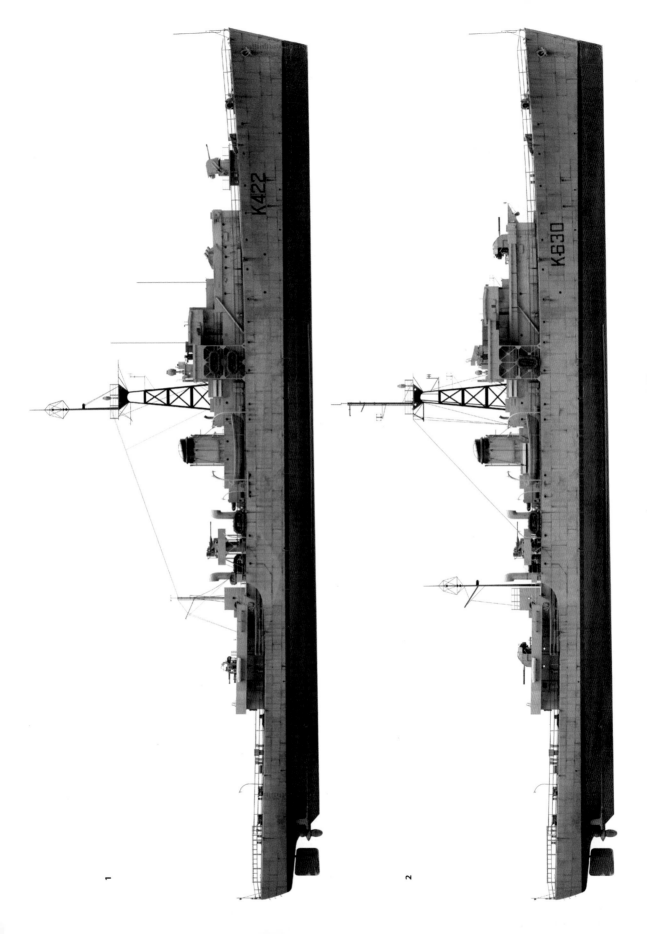

1

2

During the Dieppe raid of 19 August 1942, several Hunt-class escort destroyers provided close-range naval gunfire support to the Allied troops ashore. In the process, HMS *Berkeley*, a Type 1 Hunt, was mortally wounded in an air attack by two FW-190 fighter bombers and had to be finished off by a torpedo launched by HMS *Albrighton*.

in a variety of roles – as ASW escorts, part of U-boat hunting groups, AA destroyers and part of groups of small warships used either to counter the threat posed by enemy light forces such as E-boats or to attack enemy coastal convoys.

It can be argued that the Hunt-class vessels lacked the impressive speed of fleet destroyers, as they were rarely capable of making more than 25 knots. This made them slower than their German counterparts. They also lacked the hitting power of larger British destroyers, most of which carried 4.7in. guns and one or two multiple torpedo mounts. The difference in hitting power actually decreased as the war went on, as most fleet destroyers had their torpedo armament reduced to make room for more AA guns. Most of the latter, though, were only single-purpose 3in. or 4in. high-angle (HA) AA weapons, which lacked the fire control of the dual-purpose 4in. Mk XVI guns carried in the Hunts. Furthermore, while the first two batches of Hunts did not carry torpedo tubes, the Type 3 versions were fitted with three 21in. tubes, which gave them a similar torpedo capability to most mid- or late-war British fleet destroyers.

The real threat to the Hunts came from their German counterparts, the large torpedo boats that were built between 1924 and 1942. Most of these enemy vessels were capable of speeds of more than 30 knots, and usually carried three or four similar-sized guns to the Hunts. They also had a better close-range AA armament and six torpedoes. This made the torpedo boats useful little warships, and on paper they were easily a match for the Hunts. All the British escort destroyers had in their favour was a more robust construction and a slightly more powerful main armament, particularly in the Hunt Type 2s. The other threat to the Hunts came from German S-boats – known to the British as E-boats. These, and their escorting gun-armed R-boats, the equivalent of British Motor Launches (MLs), proved fast and worthy opponents in the coastal battles fought in the English Channel and North Sea. Nevertheless, the Hunts had the advantage of increasingly superior numbers, a steadily improving array of light weaponry and better repair facilities on hand if they were damaged.

By comparison, the Royal Navy's steadily growing force of frigates was much less versatile. They were almost exclusively used in just one role, as ocean-going ASW escorts. However, in this they excelled. The River-class frigates carried more depth charges than the escort destroyers, and crucially they also had more depth charge throwers (known as K-guns in the US Navy), which meant that they could drop more effective patterns of depth charges over enemy submarines. They also carried the Hedgehog mortar projector, a weapon which was a game-changer in its ASW capabilities. While the subsequent Loch-class frigates carried fewer depth charges, they more than made up for this in their Squid ASW mortars – arguably the most effective anti-submarine weapon of the war. However, they entered service only after the Battle of the Atlantic had been all but won.

The Bay-class frigates did not carry the Squid, but they made up for this by mounting a far more effective range of AA weaponry, as befitted their adapted role as versatile AA and ASW escorts in support of the British Pacific Fleet. This gave them a slightly more versatile role – or would have if the war hadn't ended before they could be deployed. Only one of the class (*Widemouth Bay*) was operational before the end of the war in Europe, and of the eight in service by August 1945, none of them had reached the Pacific Fleet. Still, they represented a useful late-war stepping stone in escort potential, and therefore served as forerunners of a new generation of post-war ASW frigates which would enter service with the Royal Navy during the Cold War.

Weaponry and sensors

The Hunts carried the 4in./45 (102mm) quick-firing (QF) Mk XVI gun, in either two or three twin Mk XIX mountings. First introduced in 1936, the Mk XVI was an HA gun, designed as an AA weapon for larger warships such as the *Hood*, the Queen Elizabeth- and Royal Sovereign-class battleships and most of the fleet's heavy cruisers. While outdoubtedly a good AA gun, it was also a dual-purpose weapon capable of engaging surface targets as well. Each barrel was 15ft 10½in. (4.84m) long, making it a 45-calibre gun, and weighed just over 2 tons. Its 4in. high explosive (HE) shell weighed 63½lb (28.8kg), but it was supplied with a slightly heavier semi armour-piercing (SAP) shell and a number of star shells. As an AA gun it had a ceiling of 39,000ft (11,890m) at its full elevation of 80°, while against surface targets its maximum range was 19,850yds (18,150m) – just under 10nmi– at a 45° elevation.

These guns were manually operated, but had their own inbuilt recoil and compressed air run-out systems, and the Mk XIX mounting was also rotated and elevated by hand. However, in the Hunt-class frigates these guns were supported by a Type 285 fire control radar, mounted immediately above and behind the bridge. This was a secondary battery gunnery radar, which was ideal for the tracking and targeting of surface targets. While it was also

In the Hunt-class and Bay-class frigates, the main armament was the 4in. quick-fire Mk XVI gun, carried in the twin Mk XIX mount. Although manually loaded and trained, a well-trained crew was capable of firing up to 15 rounds a minute against either surface targets or aircraft.

used against enemy aircraft, it couldn't track them nearly as effectively. A well-trained crew could fire around 15–20 rounds a minute. The same combination of gun, mounting and fire control radar was mounted in the second batch of River-class frigates and in the Bay class.

The first group of River-class vessels was given a slightly different 4in./40 QF Mk XIX gun, which had a more limited elevation of 60°. This meant it was not an effective anti-aircraft gun, but it was well-suited to engage submarines on the surface. It also fired a smaller 35lb (15.88kg) shell, and had a much more limited maximum range of 9,700yds (8,870m) at an elevation of 40°. Again it was hand-operated, as was its Mk XXIII mounting, but it had a good rate of fire of 15 rounds per minute. In the

HMS *BELVOIR* (L32), c.1943

Unlike the previous batches of British escort destroyers, the Type 3 Hunts were fitted with torpedo tubes, mounted amidships. This made these ships look like what they were first designed to be – cut-down versions of British fleet destroyers. To save on weight due to the addition of a twin torpedo mounting, the Type 3s had to lose one of the twin 4in. gun mounts fitted in the Type 2s. The aft superstructure on which the gun mount sat was moved slightly farther aft, and the abandoned 'Y' gun position was turned over to a circular mounting for a single 20mm Oerlikon gun. She had a slightly unusual suite of sensors, carrying a Type 286P radar atop her foremast.

HMS *Belvoir* was commissioned in early 1942 and saw service in the Arctic Convoys before being redeployed to the Mediterranean that summer. She remained there for the remainder of the war. *Belvoir* took part in the Allied landings in Sicily and Salerno, and served in the Aegean before returning to the Western Mediterranean. She took part in the Allied landings in southern France in 1944 (Operation *Dragoon*), and was then sent to the Adriatic to hunt German E-boats. She was still there when the war in Europe came to an end. She returned home to be decommissioned in June 1945, and was finally scrapped 12 years later.

HMS *Belvoir* – Hunt-class escort destroyer (Type 3) specifications	
Builder	Cammell Laird, Birkenhead
Laid down	October 1940
Launched	November 1941
Commissioned	March 1942
Pennant number	L32
Fate	decommissioned, June 1945; broken up, October 1957
Commanding officer	Lieutenant John Bush (until May 1944)
	Lieutenant William Shaw (until end of hostilities)
Displacement	1,050 tons (standard), 1,545 tons (deep load)
Length	280ft (85.34m) overall; Beam 31ft6in. (9.6m); Draught 12ft3in. (3.73m) deep load
Propulsion	two shafts, two Parsons geared turbines, two Admiralty three-drum boilers, generating 19,000shp
Maximum speed	27 knots
Fuel oil capacity	279 tons
Range	3,150nm at 15 knots
Armament	four 4in./45 QF Mk XVI HA guns in two twin mounts (fore and aft), four 2-pdr (40mm) 'pom-poms' in single quadruple mount (amidships), two tubes for 21in. Mk IX torpedoes in twin launcher (amidships), three single 20mm Oerlikons, two depth-charge rails aft (each with six depth charges) and four depth-charge throwers (30 depth charges carried).
Sensors	Type 285 fire control radar, Type 286P air/surface warning radar, Type I28 (sonar)
Complement	164

1. Anchor
2. Anchor cable and capstan
3. 'A' twin gun mount (two 4in. QF Mk XVI HA guns)
4. Signal deck
5. Wheelhouse
6. Compass platform/Bridge
7. Single 20mm Oerlikon (one on each bridge wing)
8. Type 285 fire control radar
9. Rangefinder
10. Foremast
11. Type 286P radar aerial
12. 'Pom-pom' crew shelter
13. Quadruple 2-pdr 'pom-pom'
14. Motor cutter (one of two)
15. Twin 21in. torpedo tube
16. Searchlight platform
17. Gun crew shelter
18. Galley funnel
19. 'X' twin gun mount (two 4in. QF Mk XVI HA guns)
20. Single 20mm Oerlikon mounting
21. Depth-charge throwers (four on each beam)
22. Depth-charge rack (one of two)
23. Propeller and shaft (one of two – port and starboard)
24. Fuel space (one of four)
25. Gearing room (one of two – port and starboard)
26. Engine room (one of two – port and starboard)
27. Boiler room (one of two – forward and after)
28. Forward magazine

The crew of a quadruple 2-pdr (40mm) 'pom-pom', the principal anti-aircraft weapon of British escort destroyers and frigates. This posed photograph was probably taken during a port visit, but it clearly shows the mounting ammunition feeds and sighting mechanism.

Loch class, a 4in./45 QF Mk V HA gun was fitted, which was an improvement as it could be elevated to 80°, making it dual purpose. It had a ceiling of 31,000ft (9,450m) against aircraft at its maximum elevation, and a range of 16,430 yds (15,020m) when engaging surface targets at a 44° elevation. This was a much older weapon, first introduced shortly before World War I, was hand-operated and had a slightly slower rate of fire of between ten and 15 rounds a minute, but fired the same 31lb (14kg) shell as the 4in. Mk XIX gun. Both of these frigate guns could only fire HE or starshell rounds.

These 4in. guns were effective, but this was especially true about the Mk XVI versions fitted in the Hunts, the Bays and the second group of Bays. Their real advantage was their high angle of elevation and their own dedicated Type 285 fire control radar. However, this armament wasn't enough on its own, as all of these British-built escort destroyers and frigates needed additional radar systems to detect approaching enemy air and surface targets. Only then could the Type 285 radar be directed towards the threat and its firing solutions calculated. At first this extra system was the Type 286 small-ship air search radar that had a surface search capability, with ranges of around 10 miles (16km) for air targets and 5 miles (8km) for those on the surface.

The Type 286 had problems though – even the Admiralty admitted that its main virtues were that it was readily available, compact and quick to install. From 1941 onwards, it was replaced by another lacklustre air search radar, the Type 290, then later that year by the more effective Type 191, which had reliable air and surface search capabilities out to a range of 20 miles for air targets and 6 miles for surface ones. In mid-1941, the Type

The 20mm Oerlikon, pictured here aboard a Hunt-class escort destroyer, was an effective close-range AA weapon. Designed by the Swiss firm Oerlikon, the weapon was first introduced into British service in 1939, but was in short supply until it began being built in Britain under licence. This Mk II version, introduced in 1931, had a rate of fire of around 300 rounds a minute and an AA ceiling of 10,000ft (3,048m).

271 set became available. This centimetric radar, with its 'cheese-slice' antenna housed in a plastic 'lantern', proved a highly effective surface search tool, with an effective range of 8 miles (13km). At shorter ranges, it could even detect the periscope of a U-boat. A slightly improved variant was the Type 272. Both were eventually adapted for PPI (position plot indicator) displays – the kind we associate with radars today. Before them, displays resembled a hospital heart monitor. By 1944, the Type 293 – an air search radar with fire control capabilities – was introduced into the Bay- and Loch-class frigates.

This association between effective HA guns, air search and fire control radars made the Hunts and eventually the Bays useful as AA escorts. The Bay-class frigates were earmarked for AA escort service in the Pacific before VJ Day removed the need for them, while the Hunts were used as AA escorts in the Malta convoys, including Operation *Pedestal* in August 1942, where five Hunt Type 2s and the Type 3 *Derwent* all formed part of the escort. Apart from their 4in. Mk XVI guns, their close-range AA armament was unremarkable. The first Type 1 Hunts carried a quadruple 2-pdr (40mm) QF Mk VIII 'pom-pom' mounted on the aft superstructure, as well as two quadruple 0.5in. Vickers machine-gun mountings. The machine gun was outdated by 1940, and was eventually replaced by a pair of single 20mm Oerlikons, one mounted on each bridge wing. Later Hunts and other frigates carried these rather than the machine guns.

The 'pom-pom' was a fairly effective close-range AA weapon, with a range of around 1,200 yds (1,100m), a ceiling of 13,300ft (3,960m) and a rate of fire of over 90 rounds a minute. These were semi-automatic guns, with the barrels firing in pairs and producing their distinctive 'pom-pom' sound.

On 19 August 1942, while engaging shore targets in support of the Dieppe raid, the Hunt-class Type 2 HMS *Berkeley* was bombed and crippled by a pair of German fighter bombers. The Type 3, HMS *Albrighton*, came to rescue her crew before finishing off the *Berkeley* with a torpedo.

In this detail of the stern of HMS *Derwent*, her depth-charge arrangement can be clearly seen. She carried four depth-charge throwers on each quarter, each capable of throwing depth charges out on either side as part of a set pattern. In her stern are two rails, each capable of carrying up to six depth charges. In between the throwers is a single 20mm Oerlikon in the ship's 'Y' mount position. Above and forward in 'X' mounting is her aft twin 4in. QF gun.

On 19 August 1942, after the crew of the crippled Hunt-class HMS *Berkeley* were rescued by the Type 3 Hunt-class HMS *Albrighton*, the latter finished off the *Berkeley* with one of her two 21in. torpedoes.

They remained in use in these escorts throughout the war, augmented by an increasing number of 20mm Oerlikons, in single and occasionally twin mounts, and in a few ships by 40mm Bofors guns, the successor to the 2-pdr 'pom-pom'. Early in the war, the standard armament was often augmented by other light weapons, such as Lewis light machine guns, usually mounted on the bridge. The need for these was obviated when additional Oerlikons were allocated to the ships.

In addition, many of the Hunts also carried a single 2-pdr 'pom-pom' mounted in the bow as a bow chaser. Primarily a means of combatting German E-boats, this proved highly effective at doing just that. Then there were the torpedoes. In the Hunt Type 3s and Type 4s, a multiple launcher was fitted amidships for 21in. torpedo tubes – a twin mounting in the Type 3s and a triple one in the Type 4s. All of them used the Mk IX torpedo, first introduced in 1930, which had an effective range of 10,500yds (9,600m), the torpedoes running at 36 knots. With such small torpedo salvos, however, the Hunts really had to launch from a much closer range. They carried a powerful explosive charge of 750lb (340kg) of TNT. Later in the war, an improved version was issued, filled with the more powerful Torpex.

Despite their versatility, these escort destroyers were originally designed as ASW vessels, a primary role which the frigates retained throughout the war. Their effectiveness at this was dependent on two things – the effectiveness of their underwater sensors and their ASW weaponry. During World War I, underwater detection relied on hearing the enemy boats underwater using hydrophones. By 1918, though, the Royal Navy's Anti-Submarine Division (ASD) was prototyping a detection system using sound waves. The physicists involved used the term 'supersonic' to disguise their system, and this, combined with the departmental acronym, became Asdic. By the end of World War II, the term had largely been replaced by the American one, 'sonar'.

F   **HMS *BICESTER* AND *DERWENT* ESCORTING *NIGERIA*, 13 AUGUST 1942**

By the summer of 1942, the beleaguered island of Malta had barely enough supplies to last another month. So despite almost complete Axis air superiority over the central Mediterranean, it was decided to push through a heavily escorted convoy in a last-ditch attempt to save the island. This was escorted by one of the most powerful British naval groups of the war, including carriers and battleships. In amongst these were six Hunt-class escort destroyers. On 11 August, the convoy suffered its first loss when the carrier *Eagle* was torpedoed and sunk. The following day, a series of air and submarine attacks was launched against the Operation *Pedestal* convoy as it steamed west towards the Sicilian Narrows. At 1900hrs that evening, the bulk of the escorting force broke off to return to Gibraltar, leaving the 'close escort' to shepherd the convoy on to Malta. Forty minutes later, the convoy was attacked again, the cruiser *Nigeria* hit amidships on her port side by a torpedo fired from the Italian submarine *Axum*. *Nigeria* was ordered back to Gibraltar, escorted by *Bicester*, *Derwent* (a Hunt Type 3) and the destroyers *Ashanti* and *Wilton*. In this plate we see *Bicester*, with *Derwent* off her starboard beam, escorting the stricken cruiser to safety while fending off an attack by three Italian SM.79 torpedo bombers operating from Sardinia. The warships reached Gibraltar safely, largely because, apart from this one air attack, the enemy were fully occupied harrying the rest of the *Pedestal* convoy. Four merchant ships from the convoy eventually reached Malta, including a vital tanker. This bought precious time for the island until its siege could be broken.

The depth-charge thrower was first developed during World War I to project a depth charge onto the beam of an escort. The Mk IV version developed by Thornycroft in Southampton was introduced in 1941, and was similar to the US Navy's 'K gun'. Although it launched one charge at a time, several reload depth charges were kept adjacent to the thrower.

The Type 128 Asdic was used in all of the Hunts apart from the Type 4s, and the River- and Loch-class frigates. It was first introduced in 1937 and was housed in a retractable dome fitted to the underside of the hull. It could operate actively or passively, and when active it was effective out to around 1,400yds (1,280m). In most escorts it was eventually replaced by the more effective Type 144 set, first introduced in 1941, which was specifically designed to operate forward-throwing weapons such as the Hedgehog. It effectively monitored bearing as well as range, and had an effective detection range of about 2,500yds (2,286m). An improved Type 144Q version followed in early 1943.

The principal ASW weapon carried by these escorts was the Mk VII depth charge. Introduced in 1939, this canister, the size and shape of an oil drum, housed an explosive charge of 290lb (132kg) of TNT, and could be set to explode at depths up to 300ft (91m). By 1941, this was increased to 500ft (182m). These were either dropped from racks mounted in the escort's stern or launched from depth-charge projectors mounted amidships. These devices, called K-guns in the US Navy, were first developed in World War I, and the Mk IV version fitted in all Hunts, Bays and Lochs launched the depth charge sideways onto the escort's beam, at ranges of up to 67yds (61m). A Mk II Thornycroft version fitted in River-class frigates had a projection range of 40yds (37m).

These depth charges were all designed to be launched as the escort passed over the Asdic target, by which time the contact had been lost as Asdic projected its sound pulse forward and to the sides, rather than down. In

The Hedgehog was an anti-submarine projector mounted forward of the bridge in River- and Bay-class frigates. Launchers contained four linear 'cradles', each containing six spigot mortar projectiles. These could be fired from the bridge, either together or in batches. The Hedgehog rounds were designed to enter the water simultaneously, forming a circular pattern. They exploded on contact, and one or two hits were usually sufficient to sink a submarine.

consequence of this, in 1941 the Hedgehog was developed, a multiple spigot mortar which could fire its ASW projectiles up to 200yds (183m) ahead of the ship. These were housed in a box mounting forward of the escort's bridge, which contained 24 projectiles. When fired, these dropped in a circle 40yds (37m) in diameter. Each projectile carried a 35lb (15.9kg) Torpex charge, which exploded on contact with a U-boat. Unlike depth charges which exploded at a set depth, this system meant that if the Hedgehog pattern missed, then it could be reloaded and launched again, without any disturbance to the Asdic contact caused by a series of underwater explosions. Hedgehogs were fitted in River- and Bay-class frigates.

At the tail end of the war, the Squid was introduced. This was a larger triple mortar, first developed in 1943, which launched a depth-charge-sized projectile up to 275yds (250m). Unlike the Hedgehog, the mortar barrels could be trained to launch their projectiles ahead or to some extent onto the beam of the escort. They were also slightly offset, so they landed in a triangular-shaped spread some 40yds (37m) apart, to ensure they bracketed the potential target. The three 390lb (177kg) projectiles carried a 270kg (94kg) Minol charge (a type of explosive suited to underwater detonation), which exploded at a pre-set depth of up to 900ft (274m). This highly effective weapon – the forerunner of the post-war British Limbo ASW mortar – worked in tandem with the Type 144 and 147 Asdic sensors, the latter specifically calculating the target's depth. When a contact was within range of an activated Squid, the weapon would fire automatically at the ideal moment for launch. In July 1944, the frigate *Loch Killin* sank U-333 using this system, thereby demostrating its effectiveness.

The Squid ASW weapon was mounted in Loch-class frigates and consisted of a three-barrelled mortar which fired 12in. diameter depth-charge projectiles weighing 390lb (177kg) apiece. These were fired automatically when linked to the escort's sonar and landed in a triangular pattern ahead of the ship. The Squid delivery system was far more effective and efficient than the dropping of conventional depth-charge patterns around a sonar contact.

Lieutenant Commander Ronald Hanson, skipper of the Type 3 Hunt HMS *Albrighton*. He was awarded a DSC for his successful destroyer action in the English Channel in June 1942, and then a DSO two months later for his part in the Dieppe raid. The following year he was awarded a bar to his DSO after another Channel action.

ESCORTS IN ACTION

It would be impossible to outline the activities of all the British-built escort destroyers and frigates described here. Instead, it might be appropriate to single out one or two of each type of ship, and to outline some of their wartime encounters. The intention is to give an insight into the types of challenges these escorts and their crews faced during combat, and also to look at a range of actions.

When the first Hunt-class escort destroyers entered service, many of them were deployed in the English Channel, where a hard-fought campaign was under way with the *Kriegsmarine*'s light forces, stationed close by in French ports such as Calais, Dunkirk and Boulogne – the nearest just 22 miles (35km) from the port of Dover, home of the 1st Destroyer Flotilla. In the summer of 1940, the Battle of Britain was still raging in the skies overhead and the threat of an imminent German invasion was acute. The first of the Hunts to join the 1st Flotilla was the *Fernie*, a Type 1, which arrived on 31 May. While escorting coastal

The Group 1 River-class frigate HMS *Swale* (K217), named after the Yorkshire river, saw extensive service as a convoy escort during the war and participated in some of the most hard-fought Atlantic convoy battles of the war. In May 1943, she depth-charged and sank U-657 off the southern tip of Greenland, and 11 months later she sank U-302 to the north-west of the Azores.

convoys, she soon found herself under fire from German coastal batteries and bombed by Stukas. She was soon joined by her sister ship, *Atherstone*, skippered by Cdr Browning, along with the *Hambledon* and *Holderness*. Others would follow, and by 1941 the flotilla would almost exclusively consist of Hunt-class vessels.

On 11 September 1940, Browning in *Atherstone* was escorting the westward-bound coastal convoy CW-11, accompanied by *Fernie*. At 1830hrs, as they passed the Thames Estuary, they were attacked by three Me 109s, but the German fighters were driven off. However, this was just a probe; 20 minutes later it was the turn of 21 Ju 88s, escorted by more fighters. Browning recounted what happened: 'The navigational position of the attack could hardly have been better chosen as the ships had no manoeuvring room. [The] convoy was in single line with *Atherstone* in the lead and *Fernie* in the rear. In order to attack the convoy the bombers had to pass *Atherstone*. Eleven of the 21 attacked *Atherstone* from the bow and right ahead, the remaining ten being held in reserve until the escort had been dealt with. In all the ship received three direct hits and five near misses.'

After describing the escorts' plucky resistance, Browning added: 'There is no doubt that the remaining bombers were dissuaded from attacking the convoy while *Atherstone*'s guns were capable of being fought.' The bombers broke off the assault on the convoy, and eventually *Atherstone* would limp in to Chatham, where she would be repaired. *Atherstone* returned to service the following January. Meanwhile, the war in the Channel continued, despite the

G FRIGATE HMS *SPEY* ATTACKING U-136 OFF MADEIRA, 12 JULY 1942

Late on 29 June, U-136, a Type VIIc U-boat, left St Nazaire at the start of her third war patrol. Her commander, Kapitänleutnant Heinrich Zimmerman, ran through the Bay of Biscay, heading towards the promising Allied OS convoy route between Britain and Gibraltar, and then on to Freetown in West Africa. This area included ships bound for South Africa, India and even the Suez Canal. During his two previous patrols, Zimmerman had sunk five merchantmen and two escorts – both Flower-class corvettes. Now he planned to try his luck in the waters around Madeira. Sure enough, during the afternoon of 11 July he encountered the southbound convoy OS-53 to the west of Madeira. Part of the convoy had already separated from the main body as it approached Gibraltar, and now the remainder were on their way to Freetown, accompanied by six escorts. One of these was the newly commissioned River-class frigate HMS *Spey* (Commander Boys-Smith).

At 1350hrs, *Spey*'s lookout spotted a U-boat on the surface, some 8 miles (13km) off their port beam. She closed with it at high speed, and the U-boat turned away on the surface and then dived. The frigate picked the boat up on her sonar, and at 1525hrs dropped a pattern of depth charges. Two more patterns followed, without producing any apparent signs of damage. Then at 1604hrs, *Spey* launched a salvo of Hedgehog projectiles ahead of her. Thereafter, air bubbles were spotted. By then the sloop *Pelican* and the Free French destroyer *Léopard* had joined in and the three warships dropped several more depth charges until Boys-Smith was quite sure their quarry had been sunk. U-136 was lost with all hands. This captures the moment when *Spey*'s projectiles hit the water. The frigate is steaming towards the contact, her depth-charge crews at the ready, while the sloop *Pelican* is coming up astern of her port quarter. HMS *Spey* would go on to sink two more U-boats before the end of the war.

During World War II, the dropping of depth charges was not an exact science. Asdic contact was lost during the crucial seconds the escort passed over the U-boat, so a wily U-boat commander could try to alter course and depth as his hunter approached. Using a pair of escorts during ASW attacks obviated this problem, so long as the flow of information between the escorts was effective.

removal of the threat of invasion following the Axis invasion of the Soviet Union in April 1941. In March 1942, another Hunt-class escort destroyer, *Albrighton*, joined the 1st Flotilla, which was now based in Portsmouth. The Type 3 joined the other Hunts of the flotilla which were patrolling the Channel, seeing a fair amount of action during a string of encounters with enemy (and some friendly) aircraft and German E-boats.

One of the *Atherstone* crew, Douglas Clare, later described what happened during these patrols: 'As there was virtually no radar in these days reliance on seeing the enemy first depended on good-old Pusser's [naval issue] binoculars. One usually couldn't leave the bridge during a patrol – the "heads" for the bridge personnel was a couple of buckets.' He added that most of the Hunts carried two German-speaking ratings to monitor German radio traffic. On the night of 5/6 May, *Albrighton* attacked a group of E-boats off Cap d'Ailly near Dieppe, successfully getting in amongst the enemy formation before withdrawing. Nine nights later, off Cap de la Hague near Cherbourg, they ran into a group of enemy armed trawlers. Clare recalled firing the Lewis gun from the bridge when the swell made him stumble, and with his finger still around the trigger he sprayed .303in. rounds all across the bridge.

On 19 August 1942, *Albrighton* took part in the disastrous raid on Dieppe, accompanied by *Calpe*, *Fernie*, *Berkeley*, *Bleasdale*, *Garth* and *Bedale* (the latter by then the Polish *Slazak*). *Albrighton* and her fellow Hunts carried out a bombardment mission, providing gunfire support for the Allied troops ashore. She came under fire from shore batteries, but continued to pound enemy positions and groups of troops spotted ashore. The Hunts were then subjected to heavy air attacks, but were still on hand to recover survivors from sunken landing craft or from the Dieppe beaches. *Berkeley* was bombed and sunk during the operation, and *Albrighton* was tasked with rescuing her crew and finishing off the stricken Hunt with one of her torpedoes. *Albrighton* would see more action in the Channel throughout 1942 and 1943, and in June 1944 was on hand to participate in the D-Day landings.

Meanwhile, out in the Atlantic, the frigates of the River class were busy protecting transatlantic convoys and hunting U-boats. One of these was the *Swale* (Lt Cdr Jackson), commissioned in June 1942. She had been used to escort the troop convoys for Operation *Torch* – the US landings in French North Africa. Other convoy escort work followed, but in March 1943 she joined the B5 escort group, a veteran formation of U-boat hunters. Her first mission with them was the escort of Convoy SC-122, which consisted of 50 merchant ships sailing east across the Atlantic. The B5 group sailed from St Johns in Canada, and joined the convoy at sea on 12 March. This was part of a major operation involving two other convoys, HX-229 and HX-229A. By 17 March, SC-122 and HX-229 were in mid-Atlantic, some 120 miles (193km) apart. Both, though, were being shadowed by U-boats.

That night, one of the convoy's merchantmen was torpedoed by U-338, having passed through *Swale* and her other escorts without being detected. This would be the first of several night attacks on the convoy. So far, *Swale* had not detected any U-boats on her Asdic. This state of affairs changed on the night of 19/20 March. At 0448hrs, while the frigate was off the starboard beam of the convoy, she made her first contact. Sub Lt Spicer recounted the ensuing events: "The RDF [radar] reported a contact at about 4,000yds (3658m). There had been several such contacts during the night, but they hadn't come to anything." Still, he called 'Action Stations'. Moments later, the Greek freighter *Carras* was torpedoed by the contact – U-666. *Swale* immediately moved in and dropped 14 depth charges, but the contact survived the attack. It was a bitter baptism for *Swale*'s crew, in what was later viewed as the most hotly contested convoy operation of the war.

Two months later, *Swale* was also unable to save two troopships she was escorting, attacked by German long-range bombers off Vigo in Spain as they headed south as part of a convoy bound for West Africa. *Swale* herself was attacked, but Jackson evaded the bombs. A hit from any of them would have sunk the frigate. All *Swale*'s crew could do was to rescue survivors from the water. The *Swale* would have her revenge in early April 1944, when she formed part of the escort for Convoy SC-156, bound from Halifax in Nova Scotia for Britain. On 6 April, they were to the north-east of the Azores when *Swale* detected a submerged contact. Jackson broke formation to run down its bearing, and fired a Hedgehog salvo as he approached.

No hits were made, so he immediately ordered an overlapping pattern of 14 depth charges to be launched. This was where a diamond-shaped pattern was released by the projectors and from the stern rails, immediately followed by a second similar pattern. The depth charges of both patterns were set for different depths; both dropped at 10ft (3m) per second in the same patch of water. The first batch detonated as Jackson turned *Swale* round for another approach. Moments later, the second pattern exploded, and this time the signs were clear: *Swale* had finally sunk a U-boat. She turned out to be the U-302, a Type VIIC submarine commanded by Kapitänleutnant Sickel. She had already made seven patrols, and since leaving La Pallice in France 27 days before had sunk two of SC-156's merchantmen. Now, thanks to the frigate *Swale*, her career came to an abrupt end. There were no survivors.

Other frigates were more successful than *Swale*, but her service record is perhaps better at reflecting the frustrations of life aboard a wartime frigate. It took almost two years for her to make her one and only U-boat 'kill' of the war, but in that time she escorted over two dozen convoys, most without detecting a U-boat. This was in direct contrast to some of the escort destroyers like *Albrighton*, which were deployed in theatres where contact with the enemy was almost guaranteed. Nevertheless, together they served the Royal Navy well.

The crew of HMS *Albrighton*'s Vickers quadruple 2-pdr Mk VIII 'pom-pom' mount at action stations during operations in the English Channel on a misty day in the summer of 1942. The two crewmen wearing anti-flash hoods and helmets in the foreground are bringing up spare ammunition. The projectiles, each weighing 2lb (0.91kg), were supplied in 14-round steel-linked belts.

The Hunt-class Type 3 escort destroyer HMS *Albrighton* (L12) returning to her base in Portsmouth after a sweep in the English Channel. Like the other Hunts of her flotilla, she mounted a single 2-pdr as a bow chaser. As a Type 3, she also mounted a pair of torpedo tubes amidships. Her quadruple 2-pdr gun can be seen abaft the funnel.

HMS *Loch Fada* (F390) was the first of the Loch-class frigates to enter service, joining the 2nd Escort Group based in Plymouth after completing her 'work-up'. Her first major task was to protect ships off the Normandy beachhead. During the summer of 1944, she participated in the sinking of three U-boats (U-333, U-385 and U-736). The following February, she sank U-boat (U-1018) off the Cornish coast.

They entered service at a time when they were desperately needed, and the crews of both ships were mainly 'Hostilities Only' sailors, who had only signed up after the outbreak of war or when they came of age. Although well-enough trained, they had to perfect their skills while at sea, either in the fierce convoy battles in the Atlantic or Mediterranean, or during the numerous see-saw actions fought in the English Channel. In almost every case, both these sailors and their small ships rose to the gruelling and seemingly endless challenges they faced while carrying out their duties.

SPECIFICATIONS

Hunt-class escort destroyer (Type 1) 23 vessels in class:	
Atherstone, Berkeley, Blencathra, Brocklesby, Cattistock, Cleveland, Cotswold, Cottesmore, Eglinton, Exmoor, Fernie, Garth, Hambledon, Holderness, Liddesdale, Mendip, Meynell, Pytchley, Quantock, Quorn, Southdown, Tynedale, Whaddon	
Laid down	1941–43
Commissioned into service	1940–41
Displacement	1,000 tons (standard), 1,420–1,450 tons (deep load)
Length	280ft (85.34m) overall; Beam 29ft (8.84m); Draught 12ft 6in. (3.81m) deep load
Propulsion	two shafts, two Parsons geared turbines, two Admiralty three-drum boilers, generating 19,000shp
Maximum speed	28 knots; Fuel oil capacity: 240 tons
Armament	four 4in./45 QF Mk XVI HA guns in two twin mounts (one fore, one aft), four 2-pdr (40mm) 'pom-poms' in single quadruple mount amidships, eight 0.5in. machine guns in two quadruple mounts, two depth charge rails aft (each with six depth charges), four depth charge throwers (each with six depth charges); 50 depth charges carried. Vessel also fitted with minesweeping *paravanes* and equipment, but these were removed during early 1942.
Sensors	Type 286 surface search radar, Type 128 Asdic (sonar)
Complement	147
Wartime modifications	
18 of these vessels had a single 2-pdr (40mm) 'pom-pom' fitted as a bow chaser. From mid-1941, machine-gun mounts were replaced by two single 20mm Oerlikons. From 1942, most had their Type 286 replaced by Type 290 or Type 291 radars. From late 1942, most Type 128 sets were replaced by Type 144 sonar. From April 1943, many Type 144 sets were replaced by Type 144Q versions. From early 1945, the quadruple 'pom-poms' were replaced by two twin 40mm Bofors and two additional single 20mm Oerlikons. The exception was *Meynell*, which had only one of her quad 'pom-poms' removed and replaced by a single 40mm Bofors mount.	

HMS *Bramham* (L51), a Hunt Type 2, pictured in the camouflage scheme she carried for much of 1942. That August she took part in Operation *Pedestal* – the most important Malta convoy of the war – and together with fellow Hunts *Ledbury* and *Penn* helped nurse the crippled tanker *Ohio* into Grand Harbour with her critically important cargo of fuel.

HMS *Brissenden* (L79) was a Hunt-class Type 4 escort destroyer – one of the pair built by Thornycroft. They were larger than the other Hunts, and better-armed too. This photograph was taken in Malta's Grand Harbour shortly after the war. The post-war '3' on her funnel indicates she formed part of the 3rd Destroyer Flotilla.

Hunt-class escort destroyer (Type 2) 30 vessels in class:

Avon Dale, Badsworth, Beaufort, Bicester, Blackmore, Blankney, Bramham, Calpe, Chiddingfold, Cowdray, Croome, Dulverton, Eridge, Exmoor (ii), Farndale, Grove, Heythrop, Hursley, Hurworth, Lamerton, Lauderdale, Ledbury, Middleton, Oakley (ii), Puckeridge, Southwold, Tetcott, Wheatland, Wilton, Zetland

Laid down	1941–43
Commissioned into service	1941–42
	Three other vessels – *Bedale*, *Oakley* (i) and *Silverton* – were transferred to the Polish Navy before being commissioned, becoming *Slazak*, *Kujawiak* and *Krakowiak* respectively. *Kujawiak* was lost off Malta in June 1942. *Slazak* and *Krakowiak* were returned to Britain in 1946 and were commissioned into the Royal Navy. *Bedale* was subsequently transferred to India in 1953, while *Silverton* was broken up in 1959.
Displacement	1,050 tons (standard), 1,580–1,625 tons (deep load)
Length	280ft (85.34m) overall; Beam 31ft 6in. (9.6m); Draught 12ft 5in. (3.78m) deep load
Propulsion	two shafts, two Parsons geared turbines, two Admiralty three-drum boilers, generating 19,000shp
Maximum speed	27 knots; Fuel oil capacity 265 tons* (* *Avon Vale*, *Bramham*, *Cowdray* 328 tons)
Armament	Six 4in./45 QF Mk XVI HA guns in three twin mounts (one forward, two aft), four 2-pdr (40mm) 'pom-poms' in single quadruple mount amidships, two single 20mm Oerlikons, two depth charge rails aft (each with six depth charges), four depth charge throwers (each with up to six depth charges); 30 depth charges carried.
Sensors	Type 286 surface search radar, Type 128 Asdic (sonar)
Complement	168

Wartime modifications

Seven of these vessels had a single 2-pdr (40mm) 'pom-pom' fitted as a bow chaser.
Before commissioning, some of the later vessels in the group had their quadruple 'pom-pom' mounts replaced by a twin 40mm Bofors mounting and up to four single 20mm Oerlikons.
By 1942, depth charge capacity increased to 60.
In spring 1943, the Type 128 Asdic (sonar) was upgraded to the Type 144Q version.
From late 1944, *Beaufort* and *Exmoor* had their Oerlikons replaced by two single 40mm Bofors mounts.

The Hunt-class escort destroyer HMS *Hambledon* (L37) pictured in August 1945, when she was attached to Nore Command (covering the North Sea from the Thames estuary to Flamborough Head in Yorkshire). She was last in action just days before the end of the war, on 12 April, when she engaged U-boats off the Dutch port of Flushing. Here she sports a peacetime colour scheme, with a red pennant number outlined in white. Note the Type 271 search radar in its lantern housing mounted on the tall platform amidships.

Hunt-class escort destroyer (Type 3) 22 vessels in class:

Airedale, Albrighton, Aldenham, Belvoir, Blean, Bleasdale, Catterick, Derwent, Easton, Eggesford, Eskdale, Goathland, Haydon, Holcombe, Limbourne, Melbreak, Penylan, Rockwood, Stevenstone, Talybont, Tanatside, Wensleydale.

In 1942, four more vessels – *Bolebroke, Border, Hatherleigh* and *Modbury* – were transferred to the Greek Navy before being commissioned, becoming *Pindos, Adrias, Kanaris* and *Miaoulis* respectively. Similarly, *Glaisdale* was transferred to the Norwegian Navy (retaining her name) and *Haldon* to the Free French Navy, becoming *La Combattante*.

Laid down	1941–43
Commissioned into service	1942–43
Displacement	1,050 tons (standard), 1,545–1,590 tons (deep load)
Length	280ft (85.34m) overall; Beam 31ft 6in. (9.6m); Draught 12ft 3in. (3.73m) deep load
Propulsion	two shafts, two Parsons geared turbines, two Admiralty three-drum boilers, generating 19,000shp
Maximum speed	27 knots; Fuel oil capacity 265 tons
Armament	four 4in./45 QF Mk XVI HA guns in two twin mounts (fore and aft), four 2-pdr (40mm) 'pom-poms' in single quadruple mount (amidships), two tubes for 21in. Mk IX torpedoes in twin launcher (amidships), two single 20mm Oerlikons, two depth charge rails aft (each with six depth charges), four depth charge throwers (each with up to six depth charges); 30 depth charges carried.
Sensors	Type 272 or Type 290 surface search radar, Type 128 Asdic (sonar)
Complement	168

Wartime modifications

Six of these vessels had a single 2-pdr (40mm) 'pom-pom' fitted as a bow chaser.
By early 1943, fuel capacity increased to 328 tons.
By late 1942, depth charge rails replaced by three smaller rails, each carrying three depth charges. Depth charge capacity increased to 70.
Some vessels had their single Oerlikons replaced by two twin Oerlikon mounts.
In late 1942, Asdic set replaced by Type 144. By the following spring, this had been upgraded to the Type 144Q version.
In mid-1944, *Easton* fitted with Type 271 surface search radar and Type 650 jammer.
In late 1944 to early 1945, *Belvoir, Easton* and *Melbreak* had Oerlikons replaced by two single 40mm Bofors. At the same time, *Easton* had Type 271 replaced with Type 268 surface search radar.

Hunt-class escort destroyer (Type 4) Modified Hunt-class design produced by Thornycroft 2 vessels in class:

Brecon, Brissenden

Laid down	1941–43
Commissioned into service	1943
Displacement	1,175 tons (standard), 1,750 tons (deep load)* (**Brecon** 1,700 tons)
Length	296ft (90.22m) overall; Beam 34ft 10in. (10.62m); Draught 11ft 9in. (3.58m) deep load** (** *Brecon* 11ft 6in. (3.58m)
Propulsion	two shafts, two Parsons geared turbines, two Admiralty three-drum boilers, generating 19,000shp
Maximum speed	26 knots; Fuel oil capacity 342 tons*** (*** *Brecon* 271 tons)
Armament	six 4in./45 QF Mk XVI HA guns in three twin mounts (one fore, two aft), four 2-pdr (40mm) 'pom-poms' in single quadruple mount (amidships), three tubes for Mk IX torpedoes in triple launcher (amidships), two depth charge rails aft (each with six depth charges), two depth charge throwers (each with up to six depth charges); 30 depth charges carried.
Sensors	Type 272 or Type 290 surface search radar, Type 144 Asdic (sonar)
Complement	170

Wartime modifications

In mid-1943, all depth charge rails replaced by three smaller rails, each carrying three depth charges.
Brissenden also carried a single 2-pdr 'pom-pom' as a bow chaser and eight single 20mm Oerlikons.
By late 1944, *Brecon* also carried two single 40mm Bofors and two single 20mm Oerlikons.
In spring 1943, Asdic replaced by Type 144Q version.

HMS *Loch Gorm* (K620), a Loch-class frigate commissioned in December 1944, was due to serve in the North-Western Approaches as an Atlantic escort, but like her sisters it was found her hull needed extra strengthening. This was still being carried out in Tyneside when the war in Europe ended. She was sent to the Far East instead, but arrived there after the Japanese surrender.

River-class frigate (Group 1) 22 vessels in class:

Ballinderry, Bann, Chelmer, Dart, Derg, Ettrick, Exe, Itchen, Jed, Kale, Ness, Nith, Rother, Spey, Swale, Tay, Test, Teviot, Trent, Tweed, Waveney, Wear
Note: another vessel, *Ribble*, was transferred to the Royal Netherlands Navy before completion.

Laid down	1941–43
Commissioned into service	1942–44
Displacement	1,310–1,460 tons (standard), 1,920–2,180 tons (deep load)
Length	301ft 4in. (91.84m) overall; Beam 36ft 8in. (11.18m); Draught 11ft 10in. – 12ft 9in. (3.61–3.89m) deep load
Propulsion	two shafts, two vertical triple-expansion engines,* two Admiralty three-drum boilers, generating 5,500shp (6,500shp in turbine vessels) (* *Chelmer* and *Ettrick* two Parsons geared turbines)
Maximum speed	20 knots (21 knots in turbine vessels); Fuel oil capacity 440 tons
Armament	two 4in./40 QF Mk XIX guns in two single mounts (fore and aft), one Hedgehog Mk XI with six salvos (forward), four single 20mm Oerlikons, two depth charge rails aft (each with up to 15 depth charges), eight depth charge throwers (each with up to four depth charges); 100 depth charges carried. Minesweeping *paravanes* and gear also fitted.
Sensors	Type 286, Type 271 or Type 272 surface search radar, Type 128 Asdic (sonar)
Complement	107–140

Wartime modifications

From 1943, four 20mm Oerlikons in twin mounts added.
In early 1945, vessels earmarked for British Pacific Fleet received an additional 20 20mm Oerlikons in single mounts.
In mid-1943, most vessels lost their minesweeping equipment, and the space used to carry an additional 50 depth charges. Those retaining minesweeping gear had it upgraded, but depth charge capacity was correspondingly reduced to 50 depth charges.
By late 1944, all vessels in service were fitted with the Foxer acoustic decoy.

The Bay-class frigate HMS *Morecambe Bay* (K624) pictured after the war, by which time she had been adapted as an AA frigate, losing her Hedgehog mounting forward but retaining her depth-charge racks aft. Her two twin 4in. guns were now supported by the highly effective Type 293 targeting radar seen at the top of her foremast. This prolonged the value of these warships during the post-war period.

HMS *Loch Inch* (K433), pictured after the end of the war. In April 1945, she proved the effectiveness of her Squid system by sinking U-307 while escorting an Arctic convoy. When the war ended, she was on her way to join the British Pacific Fleet. In 1946, when placed in reserve, her pennant number was changed to F433. Although a post-war photo, this clearly shows the location of her two Squid launchers, covered in canvas, abaft the 'A' gun mounting.

River-class frigate (Group 2) 27 vessels in class:

Aire, Avon, Awe, Cam, Deveron, Dovey, Fail, Glenarm (later *Strule*), *Halladale, Helford, Helmsdale, Lagan, Lochy, Meon, Monnow, Mourne, Nadder, Nene, Odzani, Plym, Swale, Taff, Tavy, Tees, Towy, Usk, Wye*

Additional vessels transferred from US Navy:

Barle, Cuckmere, Evenlode, Findhorn, Inver, Lossie, Parrett, Shiel

Note 1: five more vessels were transferred before completion; *Annan* (ii) to the Royal Canadian Navy, *Ribble* (ii) to the Royal Netherlands Navy as *Johan Maurits von Nassau*, and *Brai* and *Frome* to Free French Navy as *L'Aventure* and *L'Escarmouche* respectively.

Note 2: eight further vessels of the group were built in Montreal, Canada, for the US Navy but transferred to the Royal Navy under the Lend-Lease programme between April and September 1943. *Barle, Cuckmere, Evenlode, Findhorn, Inver, Lossie, Parrett* and *Shiel* (pennant numbers K298–K305 respectively) all survived the war, and were returned to the US Navy in 1946. Although Lend-Lease vessels are not included in this study, they are listed here for the sake of completeness.

Laid down	1941–43
Commissioned into service	1942–44

Specifications as Group I, apart from the following:

1. Main armament four 4in./45 QF Mk XVI guns in two twin mounts (fore and aft)

2. Additional sensor, Type 285 fire control radar mounted.

3. *Cam, Halladale* and *Helmsdale* fitted with Parsons geared turbines, generating 6,500shp, giving a maximum speed of 21 knots.

4. Fuel oil capacity now 646 tons.

5. 120 depth charges carried, but no minesweeping gear.

Wartime modifications

From mid-1944, up to eight additional 20mm Oerlikons fitted in single or twin mounts.

Loch-class frigate 25 vessels in class:

Loch Achanalt, Loch Achray, Loch Alvie, Loch Arkaig, Loch Craggie, Loch Dunvegan, Loch Eck, Loch Fada, Loch Fyne, Loch Glendhu, Loch Gorm, Loch Insh, Loch Katrine, Loch Killin, Loch Killisport, Loch Lomond, Loch More, Loch Morlich, Loch Quoich, Loch Ruthven, Loch Skavaig, Loch Shin, Loch Tarbert, Loch Tralaig, Loch Veyatie

Note: four more vessels – *Loch Boisdale, Loch Cree, Loch Ard, Loch Assynt* and *Loch Torridon* – were transferred to the South African Navy upon completion.

Laid down	1943–44
Commissioned into service	1944–46
Displacement	1,425 tons (standard), 2,260 tons (deep load)
Length	307ft (93.57m) overall; Beam 38ft 7in. (11.76m); Draught 12ft 4in. (3.76m) deep load
Propulsion	two shafts, two vertical triple-expansion engines,* two Admiralty three-drum boilers, generating 5,500shp (6,000shp in turbine vessels)
	(* *Loch Arkaig, Loch Tralaig,* two Parsons geared turbines)
Maximum speed	19½ knots (20 knots in turbine vessels); Fuel oil capacity 724 tons
Armament	one 4in./45 QF Mk V HA gun in single mount** (forward), four 2-pdr (40mm) 'pom-poms' in quadruple mount (amidships), 12 20mm Oerlikons in two twin and eight single mounts,*** two depth charge rails aft (each with up to six depth charges), two depth charge throwers (each with up to six depth charges), two triple Squid ASW mortars with 20 salvos; 100 depth charges carried.
	(** *Loch Vetyatie* Mk XXI version)
	(*** *Loch Craggie, Loch Eck* and *Loch Glendhu* carried two 40mm Bofors in single mounts in lieu of six Oerlikons)
Sensors	Type 291 or Type 293 surface search radars, Type 144 or Type 147B Asdic (sonar)
Complement	114

Bay-class frigate 19 vessels in class:

Bigbury Bay, Burghead Bay, Cardigan Bay, Carnarvon Bay, Cawsand Bay, Enard Bay, Largo Bay, Morecambe Bay, Mounts Bay, Padstow Bay, Porlock Bay, St Austell Bay, St Brides Bay, Start Bay, Tremadoc Bay, Veryan Bay, Whitesand Bay, Widemouth Bay, Wigtown Bay

Laid down	1944
Commissioned into service	1945–49
Note	another six vessels of the class were laid down, but completed as the despatch vessels *Alert* and *Surprise* and the survey vessels *Cook, Dalrymple, Dampier* and *Owen*.
Displacement	1,600 tons (standard), 2,420 tons (deep load)
Length	307ft (93.57m) overall; Beam 38ft 7in. (11.76m); Draught 12ft 9in. (3.89m) deep load
Propulsion	two shafts, two vertical triple-expansion engines, two Admiralty three-drum boilers, generating 5,500shp
Maximum speed	19½ knots; Fuel oil capacity 730 tons
Armament	four 4in./45 QF Mk XVI HA gun in two twin mounts (fore and aft), four 40mm Bofors in two twin mounts,* one Hedgehog Mk XI with ten salvos, two depth charge rails aft (each with up to six depth charges), four depth charge throwers (each with up to six depth charges); 50 depth charges carried.
	(* Single Bofors mounted in *Bigbury Bay* and *Widemouth Bay*)
Sensors	Type 191 or Type 293 surface search radar, Type 144 Asdic (sonar)
Complement	157
Wartime modifications	
From late 1944, single 40mm Bofors added.	

FURTHER READING

Brown, David K., *Atlantic Escorts: Ships, Weapons and Tactics in World War II*, Seaforth Publishing, Barnsley (2022)

Brown, Les, *British Escort Destroyers of the Second World War* (Shipcraft Series, no 28), Seaforth Publishing, Barnsley (2022)

Brown, Les, *British Sloops and Frigates of the Second World War* (Shipcraft Series, no 27), Seaforth Publishing, Barnsley (2021)

Campbell, John, *Naval Weapons of World War Two*, Conway Maritime Press, London (1985)

Friedman, Norman, *Naval Radar*, Conway Maritime Press, London (1981)

Friedman, Norman, *British Destroyers: The Second World War and After*, Seaforth Publishing, Barnsley (2006)

Gardiner, Robert (ed), *Conway's All the World's Fighting Warships, 1922–1946*, Conway Maritime Press, London (1980)

Henry, Chris, *Depth Charge: Royal Naval Mines, Depth Charges & Underwater Weapons, 1914–1945*, Pen & Sword, Barnsley (2005)

Hodges, Peter & Friedman, Norman, *Destroyer Weapons of World War 2*, Harper Collins, London (1979)

Lavery, Brian, *Churchill's Navy: The Ships, Men and Organisation, 1939–45*, Conway Maritime Press, London (2006)

Lenton, H. T., *British Fleet and Escort Destroyers, Vols 1 & 2* (Navies of the Second World War Series), Macdonald, London (1970)

Manning, T. D., *The British Destroyer*, Putnam, London (1961)

Preston, Antony (ed), *Jane's Fighting Ships of World War II*, Bracken Books, London (1989)

Raven, Alan, *Camouflage: Royal Navy* (Warships in Perspective Series, 3 volumes), W. R. Press, New York (2000–01)

Roberts, John, *British Warships of the Second World War* (Blueprint Series), Chatham Publishing, London (2000); revised and republished by Seaforth Publishing, Barnsley (2017)

Whitley, M. J., *Destroyers of World War Two*, Cassell, London (1988)

Wright, Malcolm, *British and Commonwealth Warship Camouflage of WWII* (Vol 1, Destroyers etc), Seaforth Publishing, Barnsley (2014)

INDEX

Page numbers in **bold** refer to illustrations and their captions.